Wicked
AKRON

Wicked
AKRON

TALES OF RUMRUNNERS, MOBSTERS
AND OTHER RUBBER CITY ROGUES

KYMBERLI HAGELBERG

THE
History
PRESS

Published by The History Press
Charleston, SC 29403
www.historypress.net

First published 2010

Manufactured in the United States

ISBN 978.1.59629.915.3

Library of Congress Cataloging-in-Publication Data
Hagelberg, Kymberli.
Wicked Akron : tales of rumrunners, mobsters, and other Rubber City rogues / Kymberli
Hagelberg.
p. cm.
ISBN 978-1-59629-915-3
1. Crime--Ohio--Akron--History--Anecdotes. 2. Violence--Ohio--Akron--History--
Anecdotes. 3. Corruption--Ohio--Akson--History--Anecdotes. 4. Criminals--Ohio--Akron-
-Biography--Anecdotes. 5. Rogues and vagabonds--Ohio--Akron--Biography--Anecdotes.
6. Akron (Ohio)--History--Anecdotes. 7. Akron (Ohio)--Social conditions--Anecdotes. 8.
Akron (Ohio)--Biography--Anecdotes. I. Title.
HV6795.A32H2 2010
364.1092'277136--dc22
2010041013

CONTENTS

ACKNOWLEDGEMENTS

The events depicted in *Wicked Akron* were researched from existing public records and historical and news accounts. The book was completed with invaluable assistance from historical societies throughout Summit County, the Akron–Summit County and Barberton public libraries, the staff and editors of the *Akron Beacon Journal* and sources throughout northeast Ohio—wicked and otherwise—who generously shared their knowledge and memories. Love and thanks also to Raj, the best partner and researcher ever, and to Jinny Marting for her sharp eye, long friendship and freshman composition.

PART I

EARLY AKRON

Think of it as the Wild West.

Until 1803, the length of the Cuyahoga River between Akron and Cleveland was the western boundary of the United States. The city of Akron wouldn't exist for another generation, Summit County was nearly forty years in the future and Portage Path was part of an Indian reservation.

Settlers fought the land, insects, disease and isolation to live on the fringe of early nineteenth-century society in Portage Township, the rugged frontier of the Connecticut Western Reserve. Aspirin, antibiotics and matches were all a century away from wide use. Those first residents generally lived in one-room cabins built on hand-cleared, heavily forested land with deep swamps and streams left over from the Ice Age. Roads were where you or your predecessors—trappers and sometimes squatters on your land—dug them. Keeping a fire stoked was a life-and-death endeavor. Settlers who failed the task found themselves traveling miles with a shovel in hand hoping to return home with hot coals provided by a generous neighbor.

In what is now East Akron, business took off in a village called Middlebury. By 1815, Middlebury was a commercial center of four hundred hardworking, hard-living men, women and children. Residents worked at the nail factory, gristmill or ironworks and could shop at about a dozen stores. Historian Karl Grismer described Middlebury as "a lusty town" and Middleburians as enthusiastic customers of three village taverns, which also served as stagecoach stops, hotels and "houses of entertainment for men and beast of a rather primitive character."

Though it became one of northeast Ohio's biggest industrial centers, by 1825 Middlebury's fall was imminent. Like most cities in the Western Reserve, Middlebury lacked a reliable way to export its products to the rest of the country and so was short of the cash that working people needed to pay their debts and taxes.

An unlikely, some said fantastic, solution was found in the construction of the Ohio & Erie Canal. It was a risk on which Simon Perkins built the city of Akron that we know today, and where the tales of *Wicked Akron* begin.

KILLER FOG

PLAGUE ON THE OHIO CANAL

The Ohio & Erie Canal was the engineering marvel of its day and saved the state's economy at a time when transporting goods to market meant navigating through unpopulated and sometimes uninhabitable areas. About three thousand canal diggers worked on Ohio's 309-mile project. The majority were canal diggers who originally came from New York to work on the Erie Canal. The rest were poor boys from the Western Reserve and Irish and German immigrants.

In 1827, hundreds of them are said to have perished when a plague took hold at Summit Lake that left the fledgling city of Akron a ghost town and spread as far north as Peninsula and Boston Heights. Workers blamed a "killer fog" that rolled off the lake into their tents and canal-side shanties for the "black tongue fever" that swept the camp at night. So many were wiped out in the epidemic that a saying from the time is still common among towpath tour guides today: "There's a dead Irishman for every mile of the Ohio & Erie Canal."

The acrid fumes that canal workers feared likely came from the methane created by fish and vegetation left to rot when Summit Lake was lowered for the canal—smelly, but not fatal. However, the decomposition did draw insects and contaminate the water, causing cholera, malaria and typhus up and down the canal. Nearly identical tales of epidemics

Men fishing at Lock 1 in Akron. Workers cleared 230,000 cubic yards of mud, rock and thick vegetation to build the Akron leg of the canal. *Akron–Summit County Library.*

are told about work on the Erie, Pennsylvania & Ohio and the southern leg of the Ohio & Erie canals.

The sicknesses continued to spread in the summer of 1827 after the Fourth of July grand opening of the Akron to Cleveland leg of the canal. Workers lost to death and illness caused delay after delay on the completion of the portion of the canal between Summit Lake and Stark County.

Modern physicians credit the outbreaks to the lack of sanitation, poor nutrition and immune systems lowered by grueling labor. Workers soaked to the waist dug in the muck with picks and shovels to lower the lake by nine feet, whether temperatures sweltered or neared freezing. Other workers hauled heavy blocks of stone into the lake to form the locks or hacked away through heavy swamps clogged with spiny tamarack trees that cut their flesh. Building the canal by hand was a monumental task accomplished by workers who were underpaid, malnourished and often very ill. One Canal Commission report notes that 230,000 cubic yards of muck were removed to dredge a channel through the swamp at Summit Lake, then called Summit Pond. Workers wore tin smudge pots

A canalboat on the water in Akron. *Akron–Summit County Library.*

called Montezuma's necklace to repel swarms of biting black flies and mosquitoes. The smoldering rocks and leaves that burned in the pots workers wore around their necks created a fog that kept the bugs away but left behind scars that ringed the workers' necks for the rest of their days. Canal diggers worked from dawn to dusk and were paid pennies a day, plus a loaf of bread, a ration of too-often rotted meat and generous amounts of whiskey.

Historian Karl Grismer writes that the plague spread to Middlebury, Peninsula, New Portage (Barberton) and Boston and that only four members of one Baptist church survived.

Harbor worker Ara Sprague gives this account of the typhoid and malaria outbreaks of the summer of 1827 in Cleveland in an 1881 report of the Early Settlers Association: "In two months there were hardly well ones enough to take care of the sick. For over a month, I did not take my clothes off to go to bed. I took my sleep in a chair, or on the floor, ready for the first call. People were discouraged and anxious to leave."

The fate of plague victims was often dismissed since, at the time, the proper amount of faith was thought to cure disease. As in Cleveland,

Summit Lake canal workers kept dying until there were not enough men to continue the work. Doctors bled plague sufferers, prescribed enemas for diarrhea and withheld water. "Quite understandably," Grismer wrote, "sufferers died like flies."

Akron didn't regain its lost population until the south leg of the canal opened in 1828. Most of the Irishmen rest in unmarked graves where they fell along the towpath at Summit Lake, which now is used as a bike trail.

THE HEADLESS BUTCHER

I die an innocent man.

Whispering these five barely audible last words, James Parks let a kerchief fall from his hand at the gallows to signal his own execution. It was the final act in a drama in which Parks orchestrated nearly every sensational detail. Through two trials, incendiary jailhouse speeches, botched suicide and escape attempts, Parks several times nearly escaped justice for the grisly beheading of William Beatson. It was Cuyahoga Falls's crime of the (nineteenth) century.

In 1838, James Parks was a twenty-five-year-old Englishman sailing toward a new life. A working-class man of his time would have seen America as an escape from almost certain poverty, squalor and disease that awaited him in the West Yorkshire coal mines and textile mills—or, worse, commitment to one of Britain's notorious workhouses.

As it turned out, Parks's personal escape was even more complicated. He left England with another name, James Dickinson. On the boat he shed his past as a convicted highway robber and poacher, picking up the new last name Parks somewhere along the voyage to America. However bright was the young man's dream of reinvention, upon arrival here, its actual light was brief.

Parks first lived in Rhode Island and Pennsylvania and, before long, was back to his former line of work. He was sent to prison for six years for robbing the grave of a rich ex-sea captain for the sterling silver on the man's casket. Parks was arrested, and the only part of the coffin that turned out to be silver was its nameplate—worth far less than the reputed treasure, even in the mid-1840s. After his release, Parks was again arrested for highway robbery but escaped by pulling a gun on his jailers that he obtained from a poorly searched fellow prisoner.

From this point on, however, Parks appeared to have finally, if temporarily, reformed. He moved to Cleveland, bought an Ohio City tavern and returned briefly to England to marry. It was on the voyage back to America with his bride and her two brothers in tow that Parks met William Beatson.

Beatson was a butcher by trade. He and Parks were about the same age and became fast friends, drinking and playing cards on the boat. They agreed to meet the next month in Cleveland. Beatson planned to visit his new friend as part of a cattle-buying trip to Pittsburgh.

Early that April, Beatson did arrive in Cleveland, reportedly carrying about $1,000 in gold coins. He and the new Mr. and Mrs. Parks painted the town—with Beatson's money. By the end of the visit—Parks later told authorities—both men were very drunk, but Beatson insisted on making his way to Pennsylvania. Parks said he volunteered to come along to protect his friend from being robbed on the trip.

The two men were seen together boarding the last train of the Cleveland and Pittsburgh Railroad the evening of April 13. When they inexplicably left the train near midnight and wound up at a hotel in Cuyahoga Falls, Beatson's fate was sealed…depending on who you believe either by tragic accident or murderous plot.

The next morning, William Beatson's mutilated body was found floating in the Pennsylvania & Ohio Canal near Bailey Road in Cuyahoga Falls. His head, his money and his friend, James Parks, had vanished.

Parks was arrested in New York five days later. His wife and her brothers were detained nearby. The family was stopped while waiting to board a ship back to England. Mrs. Parks carried with her $800 in gold coins.

Parks's defense attorney told a stunned Summit County jury this account of Beatson's alleged accidental death. Instead of taking the wagon path outside a Cuyahoga Falls hotel, Parks and Beatson decided to walk along the tracks at Gaylord's Grove, where they intended to flag down the next train. They left the original train car, Parks said, because they figured out they were heading in the wrong direction. Parks said he and Beatson stumbled drunkenly along the path in the dark, and then both men fell through a break in the bridge planks over the railroad tracks. Parks said he came to and patted his way along the trail in the dark, only to find his friend nearby, bloodied and beyond all help.

At this point, Parks said he "sat down to reflect." He decided that his criminal past would certainly cast him as the only suspect. With that fear, Parks said he stripped Beatson's body and then tied his friend's jacket about him like a slaughterhouse apron. Using a rock and the butcher's knife found in Beatson's pocket, he hacked away at his friend's corpse until its head and body were separated.

Park rolled the headless body into the canal and scattered Beatson's bloody clothes in the woods, darting on and off the path in the dark to avoid discovery. He carried Beatson's bloody head by the hair for some miles before he threw it into the Cuyahoga River. Sometime before dawn, Parks's attorney told jurors, he headed for home.

The local prosecutor had another version. He said Parks plotted to get his friend even more drunk and disoriented at the Cuyahoga Falls tavern after the two left the original train. Witnesses reported that Beatson wanted to spend the night in the rooms above the tavern, but Parks convinced him to keep moving.

Alone on the path, Parks stabbed Beatson in the neck as he stopped under the bridge to take another drink. Parks then stripped the body and took the money for his own. Only a beating heart could produce the sea of blood that soaked the trail at the murder scene, the prosecutor said.

It took the Summit County jury only five hours to find Parks guilty. The judge ordered a May 1854 execution. Parks is said to have taken the news "without the slightest tremor." Maybe it's because Parks knew that the verdict was far from the last word.

"I have sinned—and repented." That's the first sentence of Parks's twenty-page pamphlet published after his Summit County conviction.

"When will society cease to hunt a man down for one error?" Parks wrote. "How often is the law made a weapon…of dire revenge?"

Parks said that his dismemberment of Beatson was a hateful but excusable duty. "I shall here state, with all due respect for others, that I think it does not matter what is done with a dead body, providing that it does not injure the feelings of living friends."

As was the legal practice then, Parks's attorneys petitioned for another trial in a new venue after Summit County issued its sentence. The brochure likely was issued to elicit sympathy for that future ruling.

Parks's composure frayed as the ruling for the new trial neared. On the date of his original hanging, Parks is said to have spent hours watching a crowd of two thousand men, women and children who gathered below his jailhouse window, shouting down at those who heckled him. Fearing that "Judge Lynch" was among the angry citizens, Parks bribed the visitor of another prisoner to leave the jail with a note for his brother that contained instructions and a pattern to make counterfeit keys to the jail. Parks's escape attempt was preempted when the letter was discovered, but his wish to leave Summit County came true. A new trial was granted by the Supreme Court, and Parks was sent to Cleveland.

Parks made his first Cleveland court appearance in the winter of 1855. A new group of jurors made the then considerable forty-five-mile trip to the scene of the crime in Cuyahoga Falls, and thirty-plus witnesses from the train and tavern told their stories in court once more. Cuyahoga County's prosecutor got this rave review for his closing in the *Cleveland Herald*: "[He] begged the jury to lose sight of Parks as a husband and father, and see only their duty to the community and fellow man."

The new jury found Parks guilty a second time, and a hanging date was set for the first Friday in June. The defense asked for another trial but was swiftly denied.

In the months leading up to his execution, Parks befriended jailers who allowed him to roam freely around the sheriff's office during the day, until one day he refused to return to his cell. A particularly large officer is said to have urged him to reconsider by punching Parks in the nose. The relationship between captive and captors forever soured from that point.

Jailers foiled one escape attempt by stopping Parks's wife from smuggling a revolver to his cell. After that, Parks had no more visitors. Alone and desperate, he tried to slit his own throat and attempted to swallow poison just a day before his execution. Alive and awaiting the executioner, Parks again longed for the last word. This time he wrote a long and bitter tirade to the Akron and Cleveland newspapers that compared his plight to the trial of Jesus. "When I meet Christ in the Kingdom of Heaven, he will congratulate me...There were only two false witnesses against him. There were some twenty against me."

At the gallows, however, Parks forgave the jury, wished his wife and child well and said that he hoped his aged parents back in England might be spared news of the manner of his death. After fifty dollars was raised from the crowd for the care of his family, Parks dropped to his death from a small gallows inside the Cuyahoga County jail.

In 1861, Parks's wife sued the court for the return of $800 in gold coins found on her the day she attempted to flee for England. She lost the lawsuit, and since the heirs of William Beatson could not be found, the money was awarded to Summit County as partial settlement for the cost of hunting down and prosecuting her husband.

It's been reported, but never proven, that Beatson's "pretty well preserved" head was discovered on land near the canal that was used as a cemetery during excavation for the Akron & Canton Railway. The site is now part of the Cuyahoga Valley Scenic Railroad.

THE FUGITIVE BARBER

The Fugitive Slave Law doesn't amount to much in Ohio.
—*Marshall Fitch, former owner of James Worthington*

No one knows exactly why James Worthington decided to settle in Akron instead of continuing along the well-traveled Underground Railroad through Summit County to freedom in Canada. No one is really certain whether Worthington's beautiful estranged wife—or maybe her brother—deserves the blame for reporting Worthington to Kentucky slave hunters. One thing is certain: Worthington's would-be captors couldn't have imagined the trouble they'd face trying to leave Akron with their fugitive.

At some point in the 1840s, Worthington was running for his life. As part of the Connecticut Western Reserve (populated predominantly by antislavery New Englanders), Akron was welcoming, and many blacks, free or fleeing bondage from southern slaveholders, made their new lives here more or less openly.

By 1850, Worthington had met and married Maggie Bird in Akron, built a home on Buchtel Avenue and was one of the city's most popular barbers. His downtown shop was lavishly decorated with mahogany counters and thickly tufted, upholstered chairs. Outside, a twenty-five-foot striped pole and ornate sign advertised his location to all comers. It was that notoriety and success that would almost cost him his freedom, if not his life. Congress had just passed the Fugitive Slave Law, which allowed southern police to chase escaped slaves across state lines and required northern law enforcers to help arrest slaves who had reached freedom in the North. If they declined, police faced punishment and hefty fines. Many locals deeply resented the law because it forced them into the role of enforcing slavery.

Not surprisingly, in Akron Worthington found a sympathetic environment for a new beginning, but in the next few years the barber's luck began to turn sour. For reasons that are no longer known, his marriage ended about the time the Fugitive Slave Law was passed. Also by 1854, although his business continued to flourish, Worthington suddenly had a business rival: William Bird, his wife's brother.

Worthington would later accuse his wife of using the new law to bring the man stealers to his door. Whether she or her brother were involved is either lost to time or never was known. What happened next, however, was widely recorded in antislavery tracts and newspapers as far away as New York.

In mid-May, a well-dressed stranger appeared in Worthington's chair for a shave. The man said he was in town shopping for a house for his widowed sister. Later that night, the stranger visited Worthington in his home, put a down payment on the barber's house and promised to return in a week's time with the rest of the money.

The stranger masquerading at Worthington's house as a prospective buyer really was a member of a gang financed by Marshall Fitch, Worthington's former slave owner. The next day, the buyer and another man from the gang called on Akron marshal J.J. Wright. They identified themselves as the sheriff of Chicago and a deputy U.S. marshal. Worthington was wanted in Chicago for selling counterfeited silver coins, they said. The men asked for Wright's help in arresting him. The local sheriff reluctantly agreed.

At dawn the next day, Worthington surrendered at his home to Wright and the out-of-town lawmen without a struggle—but not before asking repeatedly and loudly for his lawyer, General Lucius V. Bierce. (The general was well known for his abolitionist leanings. In the coming Civil War, Bierce would organize and equip two companies of marines for the

James Worthington's would-be captors lost their faceoff with antislavery townspeople at this depot. *Summit County Historical Society.*

North.) By the time Worthington and his captors reached Union Depot, the barber's objections had drawn a crowd of friends and customers. To the surprise of the out-of-town officers, the crowd kept them from leaving with Worthington.

Akron abolitionist Eleazer C. Sackett was waiting for a train to Cleveland when he saw his barber caught in the middle of the roiling crowd. When Worthington's lawyer didn't appear, Sackett sent word for lawyers living nearby to come running. Two did: Ohio senator William H. Upson and future Ohio attorney general Christopher P. Wolcott. Both men examined the warrant for Worthington. It was unsigned, supposedly issued by a judge in Steubenville for a hearing in Hudson in the hands of a sheriff from Chicago. The attorneys found the paper to be worthless and said so.

Rebuked by the lawyers, Worthington's kidnappers threatened to shoot rather than give up their prisoner. The crowd wasn't backing down; they threatened to hang the out-of-towners by a railroad trestle before a shot could be fired. A reverend from Massillon remembered it this way: "I didn't take off my coat nor knock anybody down, nor do any ministerial swearing."

Rather than test the will of Worthington's friends at the depot, the faux officers left on the next train without their quarry. Worried friends and neighbors secreted the barber in the attic of another local lawyer until Worthington's business was sold. He turned up in Canada several months later, where it is said he opened another barbershop and lived happily for the rest of his life as a free man.

Ironically, Worthington's arrest might have gone without a fight if officers had sought him under the Fugitive Slave Law and allowed him to wait for his lawyer. Instead, Worthington's former owner, who was a sheriff in Kentucky at the time, concocted a false charge. Marshall Fitch later said that he had a real warrant for Worthington as a fugitive slave but he presumed the charge would not be effective in what he called the "abolition-tainted Western Reserve."

The *Cleveland Leader* newspaper reported the identity of the other "officers" of the gang that arrested Worthington using aliases. The "sheriff from Chicago" was a deputy who worked for Sheriff Fitch in Kentucky. The third man was a U.S. marshal from Ohio. The newspaper urged that the men be prosecuted. "No slave catcher shall ever carry a victim from the free soil of the Reserve. Let [the people of Akron] be prepared to apply their legal screws to the kidnappers upon their next visit."

SLAUGHTER ON WATER STREET

For God's sake, Watt, don't kill me.

Bridget Henry cried out those words three times; each call was softer than the last. The sound unraveled into ragged syllables, finally disintegrating into keening and then a whimper. Help could have come from neighbors who heard her screams so often the sound became part of the cacophony of the urban night...or from the policeman who later testified that he often heard Walter Henry call his wife "vile names" from the street on his nightly beat...or from the men at the livery stable not twenty-five feet away who walked into the snow to better hear her pleas. Instead, Bridget Henry lay alone on her own kitchen floor, broken and bleeding behind Henry's Tavern, a bar she ran with her husband. For the next seven days, she would tell anyone who would listen that this time her husband had finally accomplished what he had so often promised to do to her, and that she would surely die. "I am pounded to death," Bridget Henry told a neighbor.

Walter, known as "Watt," Henry was convicted of what was recorded as Akron's first "official" homicide—less likely because it was the first but because it was the first to take place within the city limits and was committed by a man prosecutors insisted had planned his attack and then repeated his intentions over and over to the couple's friends and neighbors.

This is what Akron looked like when Bridget and Watt Henry ran Henry's Tavern. *Akron–Summit County Library.*

It seemed like no one would speak for Bridget Henry, just as no one was willing to act when they heard her cries. Her husband's attorneys painted the forty-six-year-old as Watt's compatriot in drunkenness and, as the heavier of the pair, his equal physical opponent.

During Watt Henry's trial, his neighbors, customers and friends would paint a picture of the violence that ended Bridget Henry's life and of the culture of the time that allowed the violence. The courtroom was packed for five days of testimony and arranged in a way that would be unfamiliar today. Watt Henry's sister and nephew were permitted to sit with him at the defense table. Bridget Henry's brother sat with prosecutors. Newspaper reports noted that an unusual number of women attended the trial, so many that they were seated in a special section between the defense and prosecution tables specially created for the overflow.

Maybe the women's interest came from friendship or the novelty of the official, if posthumous, recognition of one woman's rights. There had been some talk of suffrage in Akron before—just three years before, a women's rights conference had been held in the city—but the talk didn't translate into much autonomy for the working-class women who knew Bridget Henry in life.

In their time, laws for domestic violence didn't exist. A woman who wanted to leave a violent marriage couldn't save her money to fund an escape because it was illegal for a woman to keep wages made from her own work. Women also could not legally serve on juries, speak in public or own property once they married. Churches, courts and society saw women as wives who were subject to love, honor and obey the rule of their husbands—no matter how harsh. In this era, a government calling Watt Henry to account for the mistreatment of his wife must have been something worth witnessing.

The shocking depth of Bridget Henry's injuries was described in court by a doctor who cared for her, the coroner who examined her and the women who tended their neighbor's injuries and prepared her body for burial. The hair on the left side of Bridget Henry's head was matted with blood. Her ear was nearly torn away. Both eyes were black and blue, and there were foot-size bruises on her chest, back, breasts and left buttock. Three ribs were fractured; one was broken in half. Her genitals were swollen, nearly unrecognizable.

Despite the violence of the allegations, Watt Henry's defenders argued that his role in the death of his wife fell far short of murder. "We presume that the state will be able to prove a beating took place, and may even be able to prove that Mrs. Henry died from these injuries. They can't prove there was any malice or premeditation in the affair."

Witnesses differed. They said that they often saw Watt berate his wife, hit her or drag her by her hair at the tavern the couple had run for about seven years. Things got much worse two years before Bridget's death, they said, after she miscarried their baby. About a year earlier, Bridget Henry told a lawyer she and Watt had been arguing about property. Disagreements were most likely to turn physical when Watt left the Henrys' tavern to drink at Blackie's or Huggins', leaving Bridget to handle Henry's Tavern. He rarely came home happy. Witness after witness said Bridget Henry often cried out to neighbors or passing strangers for help when Watt attacked her. No one wanted to be the first to interfere in "family business."

The night of the final beating, William Brannon said he saw Watt through the tavern's open back door. The Henrys were arguing. Watt was cursing and loudly demanding that Bridget give him a set of keys. He saw Watt pull the shades and lock the door, and then he heard Bridget scream. "There was a noise like furniture turning over," Brannon said. "The screaming lasted a few minutes."

Thomas McClelland was with Brannon and the other men at Funk's stable next door. After the men heard the commotion at about 10:30 p.m., Watt Henry appeared with a bottle of whiskey, which he passed around. Then Henry left for Huggins' Tavern but returned later that night and passed out on a bench at the stable. Sometime around midnight, McClelland said he heard a noise and found Watt's wife lying in the snow next to the stable. He walked Bridget Henry back to the tavern, oiled her lamp and built her a fire. "She sat down, and did not attempt to get up."

"'Mac, I am kicked all over, every portion of my body,'" McClelland said Bridget Henry told him. It was the last time McClelland saw her standing.

Defense attorneys said that Watt Henry was too drunk to remember the attack but was so remorseful the next day that he called a doctor to care for his wife.

Stable owner Joseph Funk told a different story. Henry stopped by his stable that night and asked for a quarter. "I told him that he had money in his house and that he should go after it." Funk testified that Watt told him, "If I go in there, I will kill somebody."

A bartender testified that Henry was in Huggins' Saloon that night telling friends, "I have keys to the house and I'm going over there to put a hole through it."

When Henry did return home, he found his wife in the care of neighbors, his sister and Dr. A.F. Chandler, who had tended Bridget Henry's wounds before. Chandler said he scolded Watt Henry for beating his wife. "Watt struck the table and told her, 'If you forgive me this time, I will never hit you again.'"

Over objections from her husband's defenders, Bridget Henry finally got the last word. The judge ruled that because she really believed she would die, the wife's testimony about their marriage and her last days would be admitted as a deathbed declaration. So through her doctor, Bridget Henry told a jury of her answer to Watt Henry's request for forgiveness. "You have threatened to kill me before," Chandler testified hearing Watt's wife say, "but have never done it until this time."

Bridget Henry died on Christmas Day. The law didn't save her, but a jury delivered a verdict of second-degree murder. Three months after Watt Henry thought he had silenced his wife forever, Bridget Henry's words sealed her husband's fate and guaranteed that he would pay for taking her life with the rest of his.

THE LOVE LETTER MURDERER

I would venture my life to give you affection.

John Henry Hunter began his long-distance wooing of Chloe Gargett with this breathless promise when she was no more real to him than the portrait he fell for in her sister's photo album. In the months that followed, Hunter and Gargett wrote each other with the sister's blessing. The couple built an imagined future from a whirlwind of words exchanged in over sixty love letters. By mid-1871, that future was an ideal for which Hunter already had killed and ultimately would die.

In the beginning, though, it must have seemed like God himself had chosen Hunter and Gargett specially for each other for one last chance at love. Hunter was thirty-one. The British immigrant had been on his own since coming to America as a teenager in 1854. He seemed to have a bright future teaching writing and photography. Yet more than a decade later, he was inexplicably working at any manual labor job he could find. Through most of the 1860s, Hunter drifted through England, Ireland, Canada, Ohio and finally Michigan, where he befriended Gargett's sister and sister-in-law and suffered a mysterious head injury that some say profoundly changed him.

In 1870, Gargett was a twenty-four-year-old daughter of a wealthy Richfield farmer. She wore false teeth and was well past the age at which her sisters and older brother had married and started their own families.

Both were reinvented in the pages of their correspondence. John Henry was Chloe's "ever-beloved and intended husband," and she was his "Pet."

Hunter's words were Gargett's rescue from an old maid's fate. The excitement of it kept her awake at night. "I could not sleep until I had answered your loving letter, which set my heart throbbing with love for you," she wrote, almost instantly intimate. "I want to see you forty times a day."

After nearly a year of exchanging letters, Hunter came to meet Gargett's parents in October 1870. During the visit, their love affair advanced from metaphorical to physical. A defense attorney explained the relationship to a jury less than a year later, as Hunter stood trial for murdering Gargett's parents: he had been "criminally acquainted with her during his visit," the lawyer said, "and considered Gargett to be his wife."

During the visit to meet Gargett's parents, Hunter spent $160 to buy land in Ohio for their future home; the amount was almost half his yearly salary. Hunter returned to Michigan expecting to be married by spring, but the events that led to Akron's last hanging were already in motion.

Trial records and excerpts from the couple's correspondence after Hunter's visit to Richfield paint the picture of a bachelor having second thoughts. In person, it seemed Gargett fell short of the promise her fiancé had seen in her photo. His first mistake was betraying that disappointment to her sisters.

"Your style suits me very well," Hunter backpedaled in letters to Gargett after the sisters warned her of her fiancé's insults. "Mary has been telling me of Orpha…She found fault because I mentioned your teeth to her…and that I spoke of you not putting on as much style as her or Mary."

False teeth, possible spinsterhood and shabby clothes aside, Gargett was still a privileged, upper-middle-class woman unused to such disparagement. Bruised pride seeps through the lines of her reply. "I hadn't near the good taste of Mrs. Stiles or Mrs. Gee. So that is your opinion on the subject, is it? I think the best thing you can do is marry one of my tasty sisters, for I do not wish a man for my husband who is more taken up with my relatives than me."

After the quarrel, Gargett seemed determined to fight for her man—or maybe just investigate him further—as she traveled to Elm Hill, Michigan, in December 1870 for a three-month stay with her sisters. While there, Gargett discovered that Hunter had left out a few key points of his own personal history.

In Michigan, he was known as a heavy drinker, was fired from a lumber camp for muttering and profane behavior and was attacked with an iron poker by an angry landlord. She was shocked to learn that just weeks before her arrival, Hunter was briefly sent to an insane asylum because of the head injury from that attack. Gargett was also humiliated by rumors that Hunter had shared her love letters with his Michigan friends and had bragged to them about the hefty dowry his upcoming marriage to a rich farmer's daughter would bring.

James Gargett told a jury that his younger sister broke off the engagement after hearing the disturbing news. Hunter didn't take rejection well. He barged into the brother's Michigan house and was thrown out when Chloe Gargett refused to see him.

During the trial, Hunter told a reporter "his girl" never broke the engagement. She promised she would marry him, Hunter said, "if the devil himself was at the back door."

Chloe Gargett never spoke to reporters and did not testify in court. Her prophetic assessment of the breakup came from one of her last letters to Hunter: "I presume it will be many a long day before you or me will forget the past. I know I shall carry it written on my heart to the grave."

Hunter returned to Ohio in mid-May. Carrying a borrowed revolver and a satchel filled with Gargett's love letters, he vowed to a friend that he would "have his girl or clean out the whole family." The spurned lover made the two-day trip from Michigan to Richfield by water, rail and stagecoach. In the village, Hunter met Gargett's youngest brother, Rodney, and offered to help him with a load of lumber bound for Gargett Farm. The two shared several drinks in a local tavern before heading out together. Hunter promised Rodney that he just wanted to apologize to his sister.

Near sundown on that spring Saturday, Hunter made his way past a dozen tall maples that shielded Gargett Farm from the main road. Chloe

Gargett was dressing for a party in her room upstairs when she heard Hunter's voice and the shot that left her seventy-one-year-old father, Robert, mortally wounded just outside the house. Her mother, Elizabeth, also must have heard the gun before she ran to the stairs and shouted, "Run for your life!" At her mother's last warning, Chloe Gargett jumped from a second-floor window, leaving the crash of the struggle behind her.

Both parents were shot in the head. Robert Gargett would linger for a few hours before dying. Rodney Gargett was shot through the tip of his ear during his fight with Hunter, near his dead mother's body, but the brother was able to run for help. In Rodney's absence, only one thing stood between Hunter's next bullet and his former fiancée: a quick-thinking and fearless next-door neighbor.

Caroline Poole was running across the field when she saw the panicked young woman coming toward her. "Oh, don't tell him where I am!" Chloe Gargett cried and ran past her toward Poole's farm. Poole testified that she continued across the field to look for Elizabeth Gargett. Instead, she came face to face with her neighbor's assassin. Hunter stood near the Gargetts' kitchen door, reloading his borrowed seven-shot revolver.

Poole asked him what he was doing and asked him for the gun. Instead, Hunter pointed it at her. "I want the girl, I want Chloe and I shall have a kiss before I die!" Hunter shouted and vanished up the stairs.

Poole said she tried to calm Hunter, or at least lead him away from Chloe Gargett, who was hiding in the potato bin in Poole's basement. Poole's children were now shouting for their mother outside the Gargetts' house, sure Hunter would kill her too.

Inside the kitchen, Poole tried to take Hunter's arm to comfort him, but the gesture backfired. Hunter pushed the satchel of letters he carried into her arms. "Read them!" Hunter shouted. "Read the letters! I have been cruelly deceived! Read and judge for yourself whether I was justified in what I have done. I intend to die by my own hand."

Poole pretended sympathy and made Hunter this deal: she would help him find Gargett if he would not shoot her, her children or himself in front of her. A group of neighbors who were beginning to gather outside followed the tense pair to the Gargetts' back field, toward the barn, stream and farm outbuildings—places Poole suggested his missing girl might be hiding. She would retell the story for the rest of her life, adding that she whispered a silent prayer that God would forgive her for the lies she told Hunter.

Hunter restated his case again and again to Poole and the rapt followers. Three men in the crowd agreed they would take him to talk to Gargett if he would put away his gun. When he did, the men jumped him, took the gun and tied his hands and feet. Onlookers could not decide whether to hang or shoot Hunter where he stood, so he was driven to Akron and turned over to the Summit County sheriff. Six months later, John Henry Hunter was hanged in a gallows built inside the Akron jail years earlier for the area's first high-profile murderer, James Parks.

In the Hunter trial, defense lawyers lost their principal argument: that earlier blows to Hunter's head had made him insane. That, however, didn't keep the infamous Hunter from going down in local lore as a medical curiosity. One of the doctors who performed his autopsy wrote an unsigned letter to the *Summit Beacon*. His assessment was that Hunter's brain was lighter than normal and in poor condition. The doctor wrote: "It is difficult to regard [Hunter] as other than a fool, who by force of untoward circumstances could be readily changed into a lunatic."

BODY SNATCHERS
OF SUMMIT

See that the Ghouls Don't Get My Body

T his eerie last instruction was given to an aide by Ohio state senator Henry E. O'Hagan in 1883. In O'Hagan's time, grave robbers reaped their harvest in cemeteries by the light of the moon with near impunity. Raids were common enough that the wary statesman's note was reprinted in his local paper to alert readers that the "cold season" was well underway. The warning meant that no one—not even a wealthy politician—could be certain to rest in peace.

It became legal in 1881 for medical students in Ohio to learn anatomy by dissecting humans, but the law—which allowed schools to claim friendless paupers—never kept up with the demand, so each new medical school session brought with it a rash of raids on local cemeteries and poorhouse graveyards. The need created big business for body snatchers and regular and sensational public reaction to the practice. Medical colleges were routinely sacked by angry crowds led by family members, deputized by local sheriffs who empowered them with legal search warrants. Newspapers ran ads for devices like the coffin torpedo, an implement designed to be buried under a coffin that would blast a musket load into would-be robbers intent on disturbing graves.

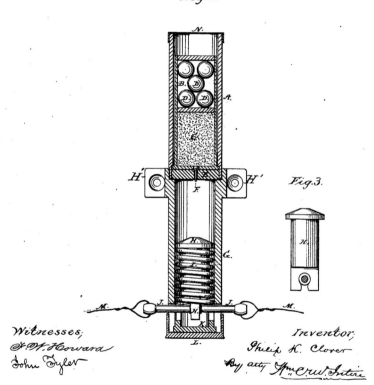

Ohioan Philip K. Glover designed improvements to the Coffin Torpedo in 1878, a device that exploded when graves were disturbed.

By 1878, more than three hundred medical students attended three Cleveland medical schools. For every five of those students, one body was needed for the dissecting table. By some estimates, as many as five thousand Ohioans unwillingly served this educational purpose between 1840 and 1900.

They were called grave robbers, stiff raisers and, more kindly, resurrectionists (by the doctors and professors who valued their services). Compensation for the body stealers' midnight harvests was enticing. Medical schools paid twenty-five to eighty-five dollars per body, depending upon scarcity of the physical crop or some unique medical value. At the time, a laborer's daily wage was less than two dollars.

Body snatching gangs cased cemeteries by day to find the graves of the freshly departed or paid infirmary and cemetery employees for the information. Since loved ones often kept an eye on the graves until enough time had passed that the bodies were no longer medically useable, removing the newly dead could require inventive work. In a common technique, the grave robber would dig a tunnel wide enough to pass through from an old plot to the new grave. He would then crawl through the hole, pry open the casket lid and grab the corpse by collar with a metal hook. Then, at the grave robber's signal, both corpse and crook were dragged backward through the dirt to a waiting wagon.

"The business is reduced to a science," an anonymous doctor described the process to a reporter from the *Cleveland Plain Dealer* in 1883, "with the aid of a sexton, the job is quickly done and not one in a thousand ever comes to light."

Although no cemetery was likely exempt, grave robbing in poor and segregated cemeteries rarely merited a mention in newspapers of the time. However, accounts of the looting of Akron's cities of the dead, from the potter's field of Spicer Cemetery to the mausoleums of historic Glendale, were plenty.

As early as the late 1830s, citizens complained that graveyards for the poor in Akron's sixth ward, including Spicer, where the University of Akron now stands, were unkept, unguarded and stood as invitations to body snatchers. However, sometimes grave robbers got more than they bargained for. In 1847, the body of reportedly well-fed local jeweler

Benjamin Tuells was found out of his casket lying at the edge of his grave—apparently too heavy for the body stealers to move.

The contest for the body of convicted murderer John Henry Hunter turned his grave in Glendale Cemetery into a crime scene almost before the sun had set on the burial party. Searching for some physical evidence of the convicted killer's reputed insanity, a group of Cleveland medical students and two competing teams of Akron surgeons each saw Hunter as a special prize and hoped to get a hands-on look at the brain of the man who pleaded insanity in the trial for the murder of his fiancée's parents.

Each team raced to the cemetery as night fell. It's thought that the Cleveland students perhaps mistook the first arriving Akron doctors for grave site guards and were easily turned away. That left teams led by physicians the newspapers identified only as Dr. X and Dr. Y to outwit each other on a chilly November night.

As the story goes, Glendale's superintendent discovered the first team of doctors as he was putting away his horse. Dr. Y's team had nearly unearthed Hunter when the superintendent discovered them and escorted the doctors off cemetery property. When he returned to make one last check on Hunter's grave, the superintendent found a second team engaged in the very same work. Dr. X, described as "a prominent local doctor," was more confident of his public standing and refused to leave until the superintendent fired warning shots into the bushes. Not to be denied, Dr. X sent for a Glendale trustee, who overruled the cemetery superintendent, who continued to resist. The groups returned to the cemetery office to argue it out. While they did, the team led by Dr. Y returned to Hunter's grave and left with the corpse. Local historians later identified the leader of group Y as prominent Akron physician L.S. Ebright. The doctor went on to serve as Akron's postmaster, vice-president of Akron City Hospital and as an Ohio state representative and state surgeon general under William McKinley.

Legend has it the deceased murderer took his last trip in Akron sitting upright in Ebright's buggy, surrounded by his grave robbers. According to the story, Hunter's skeleton was also hanged a second time. It swung in Ebright's office until the Akron physician retired decades later.

Perhaps Akron's second most sensational grave robbing account is the allegation that the doctor of the county poorhouse allowed body snatchers to use its graveyard as a body farm. Suspicions led to the arrest of Summit County Infirmary physician Alvin K. Fouser after the body of a four-year-old girl disappeared from the pauper's cemetery. The child of Mr. and Mrs. Robert Paul bled to death after fatally puncturing her lung while at play. Her grave was found open and empty few days later.

Fouser was eventually cleared of the charges, but his arrest brought a flood of allegations from residents of the county facility, which housed both the indigent and the insane. The outcry ultimately sparked further investigation of the county facility, after which Fouser and the poorhouse director voluntarily resigned.

Residents testified that they refused to take medicine prescribed by Fouser because they didn't want to die and let him sell their bodies. Other witnesses testified that five dollars was the going rate for a pauper's body fresh from the county graveyard.

Witnesses against Fouser in a state-ordered investigation of the poorhouse and its adjacent insane asylum were given free passes to leave town by the poorhouse director before they could testify. Fouser was unrepentant when reporters came calling. He told the *Cleveland Herald* that he was innocent of the charges but that he was certain that bodies were regularly taken from every cemetery in the Akron area.

Fouser continued to practice in Akron and retained his seat as corresponding secretary in a local medical association. The Union Medical Association of Northeastern Ohio had this to say about Fouser's reelection in its own publication a month after his arrest: "Doctors do not propose to go back on him…If he has done no more than the rest of us there is no reason why he should be singled out."

BEDLAM AT THE POORHOUSE

Ellen "Nellie" Towner spent most of her adolescence lying in her own waste, chained to a bed in her cell at the Summit County Infirmary, striking out at anyone who came within her reach. Towner may have had schizophrenia or suffered from some at-the-time unexplained seizure disorder. The exact nature of her illness has been lost to time, but by her teenage years, it is known that Nellie's mother had given over the burden of her care to the county. Mary Towner said she visited her daughter less as she became increasingly violent. Soon, Nellie Towner's only contact with others came on Saturdays, when the asylum's male, forty-two-year-old caretaker stripped and bathed her—and on the nights when the men from town came to Towner's cell, brought by the infirmary superintendent's eighteen-year-old son.

According to a report issued by the Ohio Board of Charities, "the Towner girl" (whose specific age was not given) was at the point of delivery before county officials noticed she was in labor. Stories from the time suggest that no one thought—or maybe dared—to free the violent child from her restraints while she brought another life into the world.

Nellie Towner was far from the first to bear a child out of wedlock at the Summit County Infirmary. The previous year, at least four women delivered children of unknown fathers. Infirmary doctor A.K. Fouser said he had seen as many as twenty strange men roaming about the

Ohio residents who could not support themselves or who were mentally ill were committed to county poorhouses. Summit County's facility was built by its inmates. *Summit County Historical Society.*

asylum at different times during the period Nellie and the other women became pregnant. He said he didn't ask about the men because they were escorted by county employees.

Despite the presence of a doctor and caretakers, the infirmary wasn't really a hospital. The name was a euphemism for the county poorhouse, a large brick farmhouse west of what is now Highland Square, built by inmates in 1864. In that era, individuals did not receive welfare or disability payments. Instead, the infirmary was a catchall for the indigent, the insane and the elderly—anyone who could not care for herself.

Nellie's section was called the "crazy house" by everyone. At night, some forty inmates were left to the supervision of one mentally ill inmate, a trustee named Tulula Rice, who said that men would often bully her to admit them to the females' cells. By day, a caretaker carried the keys that were meant to segregate the poor and ill from those with physical deformities, retardation and mental disorders thought to make one dangerous. A superintendent and his wife, who were charged with overseeing all of the infirmary's 140 residents, often went for weeks without setting foot in the crazy house.

Most people ignored or spoke in whispers about life at the poorhouse until the outcry over Towner's sexual assault, allegedly by her much older, married asylum keeper, sparked a statewide scandal and investigation. Caretaker George Keck was arrested for Towner's assault a few days after he left his job at the infirmary. He pleaded his innocence during the investigation by the Ohio Board of Charities, and his indictment was scrapped. However, Keck's testimony and the testimony of infirmary inmates and family members produced a bleak picture of misdeeds and neglect at the poorhouse, shocking even in an era when it was common belief that poverty and mental illness were self-inflicted misfortunes. Officials were accused of enriching themselves with resources meant for the needy and either participating in or ignoring an environment in which men and women were humiliated, robbed, beaten, sexually preyed upon, starved and imprisoned.

Henry Harger said he began to worry something was wrong at the poorhouse when he discovered his former neighbor locked up in the section where his mentally ill daughter was kept. "I visited the crazy house once and there I found old Mrs. Swinson, who was not crazy, but infirm, locked in one of the cells," Harger said. "She told me she was being punished because she went to town without leave to visit her son. She begged me to tell him to come out and see her."

Harger told investigators that he questioned the inmates who could speak to him. One woman said they were not fed if they couldn't or wouldn't work. "I noticed a man stealing food," Harger said. "He said they didn't get enough, but that they dared not tell."

Harger's daughter and a friend ran away from the crazy house several times, he said, but each time Harger would return them to the county. After one of these incidents, he said he visited his daughter and discovered her friend shackled in her cell, ill and hungry. "She said she had nothing but a cup of water and a hunk of bread for three days."

The woman subsequently died, Harger said, and his daughter begged him to go home. She told him that she had been assaulted in the washhouse by the superintendent's son. Ralph Hamlin swore at her when she refused to give in to his advances: "He told her she was no better than the rest of the women about the place."

Harger said he complained to one of the directors and was barred from the infirmary. He said he then turned to Dr. Fouser, eventually threatening the doctor that he would take his complaints to the newspaper. "Publish and be damned," Harger said the doctor told him. "No one will believe you under oath." Angry and out of options, Harger told a *Summit Beacon* editor of his worries.

Dr. Alvin K. Fouser was the infirmary physician for six years when the scandal broke. There had been rumors for at least as long that the doctor was using the poorhouse cemetery as his personal body farm. Fouser's trial for the body stealing of a child taken from the infirmary was postponed until the hearing on the infirmary was finished. The decision sparked rumors that the doctor's well-connected friends had engineered the arrest of the county caretaker to divert attention from the doctor's grave robbing. Those accusations were never proven.

The postponement of Fouser's trial did not entirely shield him from criticism. Resigned caretaker George Keck testified that Fouser and a medical student often dug up inmates' bodies to sell, with the knowledge of infirmary superintendent Millard Hamlin. "Mr. Hamlin told me he could get $5 for the bodies of paupers who had no friends," Keck told state investigators.

A city editor from the *Summit Beacon* said he also heard rumors that Fouser "was in the body stealing business." The editor said his paper had arranged to have some of the poorhouse graves opened to verify the accounts when the Towner scandal broke.

Dr. Fouser did not appear at the hearing to answer questions until he was escorted by the sheriff. He then denied the allegations.

A parade of county commissioners, infirmary directors and managers backed Fouser and implicated Keck as the sole source of infirmary problems in the testimony that followed, but things changed after an odd admission by Superintendent Hamlin's sister in-law. She told investigators that relatives and friends of her family bought coal intended to heat the infirmary and obtained fresh meat intended for the poorhouse dinner table. Fields owned by Hamlin's relatives also were plowed by a county team, she admitted, without seeming to know the weight of her words. "I think father paid for it," she said.

A man who worked with young Ralph Hamlin testified that the superintendent's son bragged about bringing three men to the crazy house at night to see women who were now pregnant. Superintendent Hamlin found the men there and kicked one down the stairs, the son's co-worker said.

Ralph Hamlin denied bringing in the men and told investigators that his behavior had improved. He said he had not made "Irish Ellen" dance in her cell within the last year, nor had he asked any of the insane women to expose themselves.

Allegations of treating the poor, old and ill as criminals, employing forced labor and withholding food as punishment was treatment that was not unique to the Summit County Infirmary. The practices were legal in the mid- to late 1800s. Before communities began to build infirmaries, Ohio poor laws permitted auctioning poor people—including the elderly and insane—to the lowest bidder. Auctions were advertised and generally took place after town meetings. Anyone who promised to provide room and board to the community wards could "bid out" for their labor and be paid by the county for contracts that usually lasted about a year. Poor children were sold into indenture until they grew to adulthood—eighteen for women, twenty-one for men.

Maybe that's why, despite the severity of the findings, the inquiry into the Summit County Infirmary cost Superintendent Hamlin and Dr. Fouser their jobs but not their reputations. Hamlin and Fouser submitted their resignations without an admission of guilt. The doctor was cleared of the grave robbing charge and went on to a long career in private practice. He also served as Akron's city physician and Summit County coroner. Ralph Hamlin was never charged for his alleged contact with the women in the insane section.

Newspapers loudly criticized the state charities commission for a weak final report that called for a list of obvious changes: gender specific, twenty-four-hour care for inmates, the separation of poor and mentally ill residents and the end of the requirement that mentally ill inmates work for their keep. The report also requested the end of the practice of providing medical care only for acute injuries and illnesses and of hiring a county physician based on the lowest bid.

Board of Charities secretary A.G. Byers denounced the Summit County Infirmary's care of "unfortunates" as being unfit for brutes, but Byers said care had improved "since two men were kept there in a pen in the yard." Change was not coming fast enough, Byers said in his report. He favored sending all "insane and epileptics" to a state-run facility, but he did not have the power to order the change.

A *Summit Beacon* editorial seemed dubious that any of the changes would really be made. "[There are] recommendations that can be speedily made and ought to be. The 'crazy house' at the infirmary can be made over with some regard to the requirements of sanitation and decency… Less than that the people of the county will not be satisfied with."

It was another decade before the law was changed to make it illegal to confine mentally ill adults at the county home.

PART II

WHEN AKRON ROARED

By the first quarter of the twentieth century, Akron had grown from its sleepy frontier beginnings into the fastest-growing city in the United States—a hub for both boundless innovation and every imaginable sort of excess.

The toy and cereal industries flourished here. Rubber companies Firestone, B.F. Goodrich and Goodyear were in full swing, employing so many people that there weren't enough houses to hold them or bawdy houses to entertain them—at least at first. Between 1910 and 1920, Akron's population more than tripled from 69,000 to 208,435, and more than eleven thousand houses were built. The housing boom extended to brothels, which sprung up in cities and suburbs almost faster than police could shut them down. Gangsters held sway over a thriving underground economy fueled by illegal hooch. By 1916, Goodyear began building zeppelins for World War I, and from drawing boards in Akron, the very sky was filled with miracles.

Akronites lived, loved, worked, played and fought hard in the years before the Great Depression—and even took the law into their own hands. Perhaps the city's darkest hour came on a hot August night in 1900.

This stamp commemorates the USS *Akron* dirigible. *Akron–Summit County Library.*

THE NIGHT AKRON BURNED

It was said that Christina Mass never wandered from her own front yard until the day she disappeared. Friends and neighbors searched her Perkins Hill neighborhood for hours without success. Six-year-old "Little Tina" finally was discovered miles away from home. The child cowered near bushes along Merriman Road in a thunderstorm as night approached, clutching pieces of her shredded clothing. Her feet bled. The *Beacon Journal* reported that Tina had been rescued by a West Akron couple. The wife told the newspaper the weeping girl said that a black man offered her candy and a buggy ride but instead ripped her dress and hurt her.

Akron's city doctor determined that Tina's attacker failed in all but terrifying the child. Police arrested Louis Peck for attempted rape less than forty-eight hours later. Tina identified the thirty-six-year-old African American as her attacker. Peck confessed after being held for a brief twenty minutes in the city jail. By the next day, papers throughout northeast Ohio described Tina's alleged assaulter as the "Negro Fiend." Peck pleaded guilty in a secret hearing to an out-of-town judge and was sentenced to life in prison at hard labor. The entire judicial process took eight minutes. The now-convicted child abuser asked only one thing after he whispered his plea: "I ask mercy from my God."

Above: Cleveland Press coverage of the riot. *Akron Police Museum, photo by Mike Cardew.*

Left: Cleveland Press illustration of Louis Peck. *Akron Police Museum, photo by Mike Cardew.*

Akron's City Building before the riot. *Akron–Summit County Public Library.*

Peck's prayer for divine intervention must have been granted. While a reported crowd of five thousand angry Akronites lined the streets around city hall chanting for his lynching, only a small group of city leaders knew that the town's villain was already out of reach. Earlier that day, Akron mayor W.E. Young had arranged for the town's most wanted man to be transferred to the county jail in Cleveland. There, Peck remained in safety while a mob, cheated of their own version of accountability, grew angrier by the hour.

Three city buildings were stormed in the melee that followed Peck's move to Cleveland. Local police and politicians watched the beginning of the disturbance from second-floor windows of city hall and then fled the building in panic as vigilantes rushed the front door. According to the papers, an Akron city councilman was among the most vocal in calling for Peck's head. He and a small committee searched the building and found it empty, but for a few police officers. Rather than defuse the collective anger of the group, the search seemed only to stoke its resolve. The mob moved on to the city jail, which was guarded by two deputies who immediately turned over the keys. The old courthouse was next on the list. Peck wasn't found there either, but the group suspected he might be hiding in a small, locked utility closet or behind the iron doors of the treasurer's office, the only two rooms not open to inspection.

Mayor Young reappeared, this time at the city jail. His calls for order were drowned out by the shouts and jeers of the crowd. At about 11:00 p.m., Young called the Cleveland Police Department and requested twenty-five officers be sent to help immediately. The young officer who answered the call told the mayor it would be impossible to reach anyone with the authority to send help before morning. By then, the National Guard would occupy the streets.

Akron police chief Hughlin Harrison also put the word out for every available officer. About half showed up, but even the full twenty-five-man force would have been no match for the hundreds who pelted the building with rocks and bricks. Insults grew louder as the rioters wandered in and out of the downtown saloons that remained open to accommodate them. Two men near the front of the crowd held up a mocking banner that read, "Who runs the city now?"

Around midnight, the outside groups used ladders as battering rams on the doors of city hall. As the frames splintered and glass gave way, police

Keys to the jail surrendered to rioters in 1900. *Akron Police Museum, photo by Mike Cardew.*

shot over the heads of those in the mob to drive them back. The tactic worked. Many scattered across the street to join hundreds of onlookers; even families had gathered to watch the action in their carriages. Two children among the onlookers, four-year-old Ella Davidson and eleven-year-old Glenn Wade, were killed by the police bullets. The infuriated mob retaliated, armed with 150 guns and dynamite looted from a nearby hardware store. Packs of rioters set explosives in the brick city building and threw Molotov cocktails into the wood-frame auditorium next door.

By morning, the municipal building had been reduced to smoldering bits of rubble. The adjacent Columbia Hall burned too, while rioters cut hoses and shot at firefighters. The police department's prized electronic patrol wagon was taken joy riding up and down Howard Street by rioters who left it crashed and soaked in the canal.

Sometime during the confrontation, Chief Harrison slipped out the back door of city building and left town altogether. He would not be seen for ten

Akron police officers pose at their new headquarters a year before rioters burn it to the ground. Chief Hughlin Harrison (center right) wears a watch chain. *Akron Police Museum, photo by Mike Cardew.*

days and ultimately resigned. Besides the deaths of the children, a twenty-five-year-old man died of his gunshot wound, this time a buckshot blast presumably fired from the crowd. Eighteen people, rioters, police officers and onlookers were seriously injured. By 4:00 a.m., the city was quiet.

Governor George Nash ordered martial law in Akron for most of the next week. According to the *New York Times*, this is what the city looked like when Canton Company C of the Eighth Ohio Regiment marched from the train station through Akron's downtown streets: "Electric wires, deadly to the touch, lay across the streets in the vicinity of the burned buildings. Debris of all kinds was scattered far and near…Crowds of spectators hung around, 'waiting for something to turn up.'"

What was left of Akron's City Building the day after the riot. *Akron–Summit County Public Library.*

While the militia was making its show of strength, Peck was spirited back into Akron for a hasty sentencing and hustled onto a nonstop train to the Ohio Penitentiary. Despite later reports that the train was stopped by a lynch mob in Massillon, Peck arrived at the prison after an uneventful, two-hour trip. He was not recognized by other passengers.

Peck never denied that he confessed at least twice to assaulting Tina Maas. Court records indicate that he said he was drunk and did not remember what had happened. In an interview with the *Cleveland Press* during his time in the Cuyahoga County jail, Peck said he confessed when police told him that if he did not he could expect to be tried in Akron by the same citizens who had burned part of the city to get their hands on him.

Whether Peck confessed out of guilt or fear of mob justice is not clear, and neither is his background. Reports of his past crimes and personal details were ascribed to both Lewis and Louis Peck, thirty-six and forty years old, who was reported simultaneously by competing newspapers to be a Garrettsville farmer, an Akron restaurant worker, a Cleveland dockworker and a wanted child abuser from Paterson, New Jersey. Because there was no trial, there also was no good investigation of why Peck would leave the city after committing the crime only to return to a train station in the middle of town where he was actively being sought by virtually every man, woman and child.

Contemporary readers may wonder about Akron's racial mindset during those days. Was the city an antislavery hub on the Underground Railroad that rescued escaped slave James Worthington from his accusers and supported abolitionist John Brown, or was it a haven for lynch-lusting racists?

Likely, it was both.

Writers of post-riot editorials and letters wrestled in the same newspapers that indicted Peck to understand citizens who could behave at such extremes. Leaders did go to extraordinary lengths to protect a black man accused of a horrific offense. Yet a good number of Akron's citizens were ready to kill Peck without benefit of the legal process or reasonable proof of his guilt. Depending on the post–Civil War viewpoint of respective newspaper publishers, Peck was a catalyst for a city that had either shamed itself by succumbing to temporary insanity or had finally come to its senses regarding race in the attempted lynching.

In the local courts, more than thirty of the forty people arrested for taking part in the riot were prosecuted. A local prosecutor refused to go after the rest after the councilman who was involved in the riot received a light sentence.

Louis Peck served thirteen years of his life sentence in the Ohio Penitentiary before being pardoned. Little is known about the details of his incarceration beyond its beginning and end. Peck spent the first thirty days in solitary confinement. The last five years of custody Peck was a servant in the home of Warden T.H.B. Jones.

In May 1913, Peck was released by Ohio governor James M. Cox on the condition that he leave the state to accept work in West Virginia. In the pardon, Cox wrote that Peck could not have proved his innocence in the brief hearing, in which he was not represented by an attorney. A letter from Akron city doctor A.K. Fouser that stated that Tina Maas had not been sexually assaulted also helped free Peck, as did the recommendation of Warden Jones.

AKRON'S FIRST GODFATHER

Rosario Borgia often cried in his cell late at night. Electrical storms reduced him to panicked shrieking that echoed off the bars. It was hardly the way anyone expected Akron's king of organized crime to behave, but by then, Borgia knew he would die in Ohio's electric chair before his twenty-sixth birthday.

Some said the burly young Sicilian once wrestled for his supper, but by 1912, Borgia ruled Akron's North Hill from his general store on Furnace Street. He bragged that the self-made fortress was "police proof." The pretension of invincibility wasn't limited to the many politicians and police he allegedly had on his payroll. Practically the only fortification missing from Borgia's store was a moat. Both doors were alarmed, and deep pits were dug beneath the front and back stairs. Pull a switch and the young capo's enemies met their maker at the points of steel spikes buried in the ground a floor below. A trapdoor to the basement concealed an arsenal stowed in a secret room where criminals on the lam paid to wait out police. After hours, Borgia often stayed in the apartment above his store, which doubled as the local bordello. He also had rooms at the Buchtel Hotel—where he was ultimately arrested for the contract murder of four Akron police officers.

From the store, Borgia led a diversified criminal empire of bootlegging, blackmail, dope peddling and prostitution. Those who weren't customers

Rosario Borgia was
executed for ordering
the murders of four
Akron police officers.
Ohio Historical Society.

of his illegal goods often paid protection money to ensure the health of
their families and businesses. By 1916, the criminal entrepreneur had
become the merciless fist of Akron's Black Hand Society. A forerunner
of the Mafia, the Black Hand was the largest organized crime gang in
the Midwest in its day—and Borgia ran it largely unrestrained by the law.

His success might have gone on indefinitely but for one fatal mistake.
Like all successful business owners, Borgia wanted to expand.

Who could blame him? Akron was bursting at its seams. Production in
the rubber companies was at an all-time high, thanks to wartime demand
for tires, gas masks, blimps and balloons. Local companies spent millions

to add additions that dwarfed their original plants. To staff those growing factories, more men were needed—many more than anyone would ever have imagined.

Waves of workers came north to fill fifty thousand spots on Akron assembly lines—double the number employed just three years before. In many ways, the supply of labor far outstripped the city's ability to accommodate them. Beds were rented to single men by eight-hour shifts in the attics, basements, garages and even chicken coops of enterprising Akronites. Shantytowns sprung up at the outskirts of the city. Rubber workers could make an astounding five to seven dollars a day—more than most other industries paid in a week. Even those who sent most of their pay home to struggling families on the farm had plenty left over. For Borgia, there was no better market than the hordes of willing, restless young men milling about the city with full wallets and little to occupy their off hours.

After less than a decade in business, there was hardly a bottle of backroom brew or a woman working Akron's streets that he did not control. Those who found some measure of success through more conventional methods beyond the boundaries of North Hill were now within Borgia's reach. Akronites of all stripes lived in dread of finding a demand for cash marked with the ink-stained palm that gave the Black Hand Society its menacing nickname.

Borgia saw himself as meeting a growing public demand. It was his version of achieving the American Dream, but his success had an unintended consequence. Fleecing a mark in a crooked card game, blackmailing a John for his visits to a bawdyhouse or shaking down a store owner caused little concern when the victims were confined to the poor of North Hill. When those victims started coming from Akron's burgeoning wartime workforce, and even its elite, Borgia found that he had become a target.

By 1917, he could hardly leave Furnace Street without seeing an Akron police officer on his tail. Gang members grumbled to Borgia that the constant patrols made it tough to make a living. Though no one put the two occurrences together right away, it also was about the same time that Akron police officers began to die on duty.

A gun used in contract mob hits on four Akron policemen. *Akron Police Museum, photo by Mike Cardew.*

Accounts of the ambush of Officers Guy Norris, Edward J. Costigan, Joseph Hunt and Gethin Richards have been given in the *Beacon Journal*, a handful of pulp detective magazines, confessions of two Borgia gang members and the autobiography of at least one of the arresting officers. What follows is a chronology of details that are common to each account.

Patrolman Norris was walking his beat at High and Market Streets two days before Christmas when he saw what looked like a robbery. Norris ran into the dark alone and grabbed the supposed robber. Instead of fleeing, the would-be victim attacked the officer, who was shot repeatedly in the back. Norris died on Christmas Eve without identifying his killers. Three weeks later, Officers Costigan and Hunt were ambushed using the same trick. Costigan died immediately, but Hunt managed to run, despite being shot several times. He lingered for days at Akron General (then People's) Hospital, surrounded by fellow officers who waited in vain for Hunt to regain consciousness and identify his attacker.

Throughout the winter, the Borgia gang continued to run much of the crime in Akron while police struggled with an investigation that seemed to have run cold. Detectives were at a loss for a motive, and since the shootings occurred in different areas of the city, no one believed the murders were related.

Then, come spring of 1918, another patrolman was gunned down. Officer Gethin Richards saw three suspicious-looking men near the railroad tracks. With a passerby named George Fink, he followed the men into an alley and ordered them to throw up their hands. While Richards was busy searching one man for weapons, another fired three times. As Richards fell, everyone scattered. Fink ran to summon police, who quickly arrested Frank Mazzano and Paul Chiavaro hiding in the railroad yard. Richards died, but not before he had identified his killers.

Mazzano confessed to his part in the Richards shooting almost immediately, but he had another more shocking story to tell: the murders of all four officers were connected. "Borgia paid $100 each for Hunt and Costigan," Mazzano said, "paid them in his cellar. I saw him pay the money."

Mazzano also painted a vivid picture of Borgia's hatred of police in his description of Richards's death. The pair waited for Richards in the dark together, Mazzano said. Borgia jumped the officer from behind. When Richards was helpless, Borgia ordered Mazzano to shoot.

Borgia and five gang members implicated in the mob hits on police were jailed and indicted within two weeks of the confession. Borgia, Mazzano and two others received the death penalty.

Waiting out a series of appeals to his conviction, Borgia became the Summit County Jail's version of Scheherazade, regularly confessing to a string of crimes he hoped would delay his visit to Ohio's electric chair. The most sensational of those confessions was the unsolved murder and mutilation that police dubbed the Triplett Road Murder.

Borgia told investigators that he was paid to have a member of his gang kill a young stranger over money and jewelry lost in a North Hill card game. At issue was a gold watch chain. The young winner, an out-of-towner no one seemed to know, refused to give or sell back the jewelry. Borgia took the job for $100. The chain was returned to the client, but Borgia said his men demanded $150. The price hike, he told police, was due to the unexpected difficulty of the job. One of the detectives later related Borgia's story to the *Cleveland Press* this way: "When you have to kill a guy, it's worth more." Once it was made clear to Borgia's client that he might live to haggle again only by paying the higher rate, the deal was done.

The card winner's body was found sprawled halfway out of a basement door on Triplett Boulevard by a boy hunting for mushrooms in an adjacent field. Police said the man—who was never identified by name—was likely Italian or Greek and about eighteen years old. He was found rolled in a blood-spattered sheet. When the body was more closely examined, police found feathers clinging to the man's clothing, and his genitals had been sliced off.

Borgia wasn't charged with the new murder. He and Mazzano were executed at the Ohio Penitentiary for killing Akron police officer Gethin Richards on February 21, 1919. The men died within minutes of each other, just before midnight, before more than one hundred Akron witnesses.

Borgia lost control of his legs at the sight of Mazzano's body being carried from the death chamber in a wicker basket (his body reportedly still smoked from the heat of the electrocution). The former mob boss had to be supported by a guard under each arm as he made his last walk.

Protesting to the last, Borgia told witnesses that he should receive a lesser penalty because he merely ordered the murders that others committed. "I don't think it right for me to die," Borgia said. "I am innocent."

The *Beacon Journal* described the men's last moments in detail. Mazzano died well, the paper said, walking to the electric chair under his own power after telling Summit sheriff James A. Corey, "Send my regards to the boys." Mazzano, "the game one," required three jolts over sixty seconds, according to the *Beacon Journal*. Borgia, "the yellow-streaked one," died in twenty seconds.

Two weeks after the executions, three more Akron police officers were shot on patrol. Officer George Werne died, but patrolmen Steve McGowan and William McDonald, though wounded, managed to return fire and injure two of three assailants, all Borgia gang members.

Fifteen years after Borgia ordered the killings of Norris, Hunt, Costigan and Richards, gang member Lorenzo Biondo's life sentence was secretly commuted by Ohio governor George White. Biondo fled to Italy, and all records of his release mysteriously disappeared.

THE BAD GUYS
WORE WHITE

Invisible behind a sea of white hoods and flowing robes, thousands marched down Akron's Main Street and set suburban hillsides alight with flaming crosses.

Ku Klux Klan activity began in the Akron area in 1921, but the organization didn't really gain a local foothold until a year later. The Summit County Klan of the 1920s turned blind bigotry against African Americans, Jews, Catholics, Irish and Greeks into virtually ubiquitous institutional power. Who got elected, who went to jail, whether businesses failed or thrived, even how Akron worshipped and what its students learned in public schools was largely controlled by the group, which had a large Women's Auxiliary, a junior division for teenage boys, a band and even a glee club. The Summit KKK was ranked as the largest regional branch in the United States by its national headquarters. By 1923, fifty-two thousand locals were members—one-quarter the population of Akron at the time, or enough to fill the modern-day University of Akron football stadium twice over.

In some ways, Greater Akron was a predictable spot for the Klan to succeed in the North. Irish and Italian immigrants came here in increasing numbers, along with African Americans and southern whites. White Protestants feared they would be displaced as the top immigrant group sought by the local factories. When Klan members boasted that

Summit County Ku Klux Klan Women's Auxiliary members aboard their float in Akron's centennial parade. *Akron–Summit County Public Library.*

only their exclusively white, Protestant membership could claim to be "100 Percent American," and thus worthy of those jobs, the rallying cry met a receptive and threatened audience.

As the Klan became an essential "in group" for jobseekers, Klan membership also paid off for its leaders, who operated openly in the community. Summit's first exalted Cyclops, E.E. Zesiger, became an Akron Municipal Court judge. He was followed by Joseph "J.B." Hanan, who worked nearly three decades as a manager for B.F. Goodrich. Hanan went on to serve as a Kent State University trustee and president of the Akron School Board. At various times in the 1920s, the Summit KKK counted Akron's mayor, superintendent of schools, the sheriff, county commissioners, the county prosecutor, members of city council and the majority of Hanan's school board among its members. So many of the "Invisible Empire" served in the local branch of the National Guard that the group was nicknamed the "Grand Dragon's Guard."

The Klan's hold on Akron came about through a sophisticated drive for local hearts and minds that included regional and state conventions held

J.B. Hanan, Akron School Board president and Summit County KKK exalted Cyclops. *Akron* Beacon Journal.

here, church demonstrations and perhaps the pinnacle show of influence, the 1923 parade. The spectacle shut down traffic on Main and Exchange Streets. Onlookers gawked at thousands of marchers on the ground as a crop-dusting plane rimmed with red lights swooped above, looking to all the world like a fiery airborne cross. Local preachers acted as emcees at a picnic and fireworks display that followed at a city park. More than twelve thousand faithful "Hundred Percenters" listened to KKK leaders make their pitch and checked out displays from local merchants, student groups and politicians. Ohio grand dragon Clyde Osborne boasted of the Klan's growing statewide power. The message was clear: join or be left out in the cold.

National religious headliners added to the Klan's local muscle. Evangelist Bob Jones, who later founded the racially exclusionist Bob

Akron Ku Klux Klan members distribute Christmas gifts. *Akron* Beacon Journal.

Jones University in Greenville, South Carolina, spoke at outdoor revivals in Akron and across the country flanked by the KKK's iconic flaming cross. At his Goodyear Park appearance, however, Jones mixed racist rhetoric with an image more in keeping with the city's status as the early twentieth-century home of high-tech inventors and rubber barons. The cross was electrified, three stories tall and cast a red glow across acres of rubber plant housing.

At Goodyear Park, Jones preached the KKK gospel and was covered word for word the next day in the *Beacon Journal*: "When you speak of white supremacy you say that you are against colors mixing and I'm with you on that."

His warning about the dangers of voting for non-Protestants received an enthusiastic ovation. "We don't have popes and kings over here. We're all common people. We don't send anyone from Washington to the Vatican and we don't want anyone from the Vatican to be sent over here."

Summit church leaders echoed the marriage of Protestant church and state from their pulpits, and the Klan showed its appreciation. Churches voted en masse for Klan-approved candidates, and on Sundays, large groups of KKK members routinely showed up at churches to deliver fat donations. The church gifts usually were given with great ceremony. One hundred or so hooded men would interrupt a service by lining the aisles and then marching silently past the pews to the pulpit. Klan members rarely spoke or identified themselves after handing over the cash, and they left the church in cars that did not bear license plates.

By Easter, grateful worshippers in white Protestant churches were regularly holding Klan-only services and espousing philosophies that were, at minimum, anti-ecumenical.

In black churches, the sight of a gang of one hundred or so masked white men marching into the sanctuary was intimidating and clear. The head of an African American Baptist church in Wadsworth told the *Beacon Journal* that his church had been visited by the Klan and that he intended to keep the money. After the report, the church doesn't appear in the newspaper's index. That doesn't mean it disappeared because of the KKK. However, it's interesting to note that the city, on the Summit/Medina County border, evolved to become over 97 percent white, well below the statewide average.

Over the next two years, the Summit Klan began to reach outside the pulpit. Flaming crosses once used to signal local meetings started turning up in African American, Catholic and Jewish sections of town. Immigrants who attended night school to learn English at a local elementary school watched from their windows as a large cross burned in protest in a lot across the street.

Businesses were pressured not to hire or do business with nonmembers, and those who were affected by the prejudice rarely complained. It was three years after the fact that such an incident was described in the newspaper, and still the writer chose anonymity. "A colored citizen" wrote to the editor that he faced discrimination from supervisors who were Klan members. The man said he was fired after he disagreed with

I pledge allegiance to the Klan… KKK members presented cash, flags and Bibles to county churches and schools. *Akron Beacon Journal.*

a new boss about Klan policy. The writer said his dismissal came after two years on the job with men of different races. "I am colored and not a hypocrite, and would not admit that the Klan was good for me."

Opposition in court from Akron's prominent Jewish leaders and the NAACP managed only to interrupt the occasional publicized Klan meeting on city or state property. By 1924, with many in Akron's business, religious and political communities behind it, the group set its sights on the last piece of the puzzle—control of Akron's public schools.

As they had in churches, hooded Klansmen began turning up at city and suburban schools. This time the presentations included gifts of the

American flag and a copy of the Holy Bible—the version of the book used in Protestant worship. Before long, the school board—still led by local Klan leader J.B. Hanan—won forced compulsory Bible reading classes in the schools, using the Bible that flouted the beliefs of Catholic and Jewish schoolchildren.

In January, Akron's well-regarded school superintendent Carroll Reed resigned with three years left on his contract, along with three anti-Klan board members. The *Beacon Journal* headline, "Klan Now in Control," signaled a 4–3 KKK majority on the school board. A few months later, Hanan pressed that advantage to hire George McCord, a Klan member handpicked by state KKK leaders as Akron's new school superintendent.

McCord was the former leader of southern Ohio's Springfield School District. In Springfield, he defied a federal court order to keep black and white elementary students segregated. When the plan for a Jim Crow school failed, McCord immediately fired forty black teachers and school administrators rather than allow them to supervise white children. A raid on Springfield's Klan headquarters during the yearlong boycott of the school revealed that McCord worked with politicians who were Klan

A Klan march in Akron schools superintendent/KKK member George McCord's old district near Dayton. *Ohio Historical Society.*

members to deny food aid and other social services to black families who opposed him in his school plan.

Opponents of McCord's hiring said that the superintendent had sneaked into Akron schools—under a sheet. At least initially, those who opposed the Klan's education policies in 1925 were armed with little more than clever insults.

Once hired, McCord moved quickly to extend his influence to the business community. As in Springfield, he took over as the district's purchasing agent. Klan standing became a prerequisite for virtually all school jobs and purchases. McCord's son and other KKK associates were given jobs without the required civil service test. The Klan school board majority simply voted to change the rules when the new hires were criticized. Then, echoing his practice in Springfield and the grand dragon's promise in an Akron speech, McCord moved to fire the district's Catholic teachers.

The changes sparked a vocal public war for control of the schools waged in the months leading up to the November election by the anti-Klan Non-Political School League (NPL) and the Citizens League, made up of Hanan and McCord loyalists. Both sides claimed secret meetings and dirty dealings. Each side published its own newspaper and heckled its challenger's public meetings, and one side enlisted the help of a future presidential candidate.

The NPL was supposedly hatched with backing from the chamber of commerce in secret meetings at the Akron City Club after Carroll Reed's assistant superintendent was passed over for superintendent and subsequently resigned. The group lobbied heavily in the immigrant community.

NPL leaders argued that a vote for any school board incumbent was a vote for the Klan, which boasted control of seven school boards across Ohio. The NPL concentrated its efforts on increasing voter registration in poor and immigrant neighborhoods.

Years before Wendell Wilkie became the Republican Party's presidential candidate, he was an active Democrat who came to work as a lawyer for Firestone Tire and Rubber Company. While in Akron, he also championed the NPL's cause. Wilkie spoke against Klan control of the schools to anyone who would listen, and as a delegate to the

"Save Our Schools"

Non-Political Public School League

306 METROPOLITAN BUILDING

PHONE MAIN 5561

AKRON, O.,   September 28, 1925

Dear Friend:

Our active campaign for liberating our School
Board from Ku Klux Klan control commences on the first
day of registration, - October 1st. - next Thursday.

We already have your assurance of sympathy and
offer of support in this movement.

In order to give us the necessary co-operation
it is absolutely imperative that you go to the polls
Thursday, October 1st and register.

Every voter must register - no previous registration counts. Booths are open from 8:00 A.M. to 2:00
P.M. and from 4:00 P.M. to 9:00 P.M.

As a further effort, I want to suggest that you
register as early as possible and then call up your neighbors and friends and see if they, too, have registered;
if not, urge them to go to the polls. Use the telephone
freely and contact with every one of your friends. In
this way you can be of help and assistance.

This is a crisis in the city's affairs and in
order to save our schools we need your help.

Very truly yours,

E. E. Helm
MAR.

Campaign letter from a group opposed to KKK school board candidates. *Akron* Beacon Journal.

Democratic National Convention a year earlier, he had worked hard—
and unsuccessfully—to get the party to repudiate the KKK in its official
platform. When news of his efforts reached the Summit Klan, the story
goes that Wilkie received a telegraph asking when he had joined the
"payroll of the Pope." Wilkie sent back this locally famous six-word reply:
"The Klan can go to hell."

During the summer of 1925, Wilkie is said to have practically given up his law practice to speak against Klan control of the school board. "This man Hanan has thrown down the challenge that he controls the city," Wilkie said, according to the *Beacon Journal*. "Let me take it up and fight it out. I do not think he does."

Wilkie's message resonated among the city's non-Protestant, African American and immigrant citizens, but whether the city's majority was ready for a change was still uncertain.

The Klan marched in the city's centennial parade a month later. A float by the KKK women's group was prominently displayed, led by McCord's wife, who was the group's president.

Members of the Citizens League, who were also school board members, also had a lot to say in the run-up to the election. Board member Ruby Kahlor warned voters at one campaign meeting that "all immortality lies at the door of the foreign born."

Hanan criticized the NPL for printing campaign literature in five languages but assured the audience that he had nothing against a foreigner who can't read English. Hanan said he refused an order from the chamber of commerce to hire Reed's successor. He said the chamber relayed its message from a secret meeting at the City Club: vote their way or the chamber would go after the Klan. Hanan said NPL candidates were beholden to their own leader, whom they had promised to pay thousands after the election.

The Home and School League, made up of Catholic, Jewish and Protestant mothers, declined to endorse either side.

After a recount in which an NPL candidate gained thirteen votes, the election ended in a tie. Both sides claimed victory. Three of Wilkie's anti-Klan candidates were elected, along with three of Hanan's pro-Klan incumbents. The swing vote on the board was retained by an incumbent who was originally appointed by Hanan but who claimed neutrality during the election.

It was the first Akron election in which a candidate that was endorsed by the Klan was not elected.

A year later, Hanan resigned his Klan post, and anti-Klan candidates held a majority on the board. In 1927, George McCord's contract as superintendent was not renewed. It was his last job in an Ohio school district.

THE BATTLE OF LAKE ANNA

The boundless capitalism that turned Summit County into one of the fastest-growing industrial regions in the country in the early 1900s was hobbled by the Great Depression. In 1931, a report by the chamber of commerce estimated more than 20 percent of Akron's industrial workforce was jobless. One thousand unemployed residents marched on city hall that January to unsuccessfully demand a weekly stipend of twenty-five dollars. Soup kitchens were a new staple in the area.

Factories throughout Summit County slashed work hours to avoid layoffs, but the cuts came anyway. Mistrust grew between companies that continued to post (albeit meager) profits and the workers who left their homes and families for jobs that no longer existed.

One of the byproducts of the economic strife was an increased interest in Communism. Party members found a receptive audience in the thousands of suddenly disenfranchised workers who flocked to protest speeches. Initially, city governments saw the speeches as a safety valve for growing frustration and readily gave permission for the groups to meet in free venues like public parks. As the number of jobless grew, however, companies began locking their doors against throngs of desperate jobseekers who showed up each day. The unease spread to some city governments that banned the meetings as a likely threat to public safety.

At the same time in Barberton, more than half the city's main wage earners were out of work. Those who were lucky enough to have jobs suffered low wages and poor working conditions. Barberton's unemployed were becoming increasingly more vocal. One of the most vocal was a thirty-one-year-old African American named C. Louis Alexander, a Communist labor organizer who was working with a group of unemployed Barbertonians. Neighbors said that Alexander vanished after being beaten by two Barberton police officers. Police had no record of his arrest. Perhaps more worrisome was a complaint from witnesses that "men in uniforms" were seen after the disappearance throwing a large box into a lake down by the factories.

Alexander had fled to relatives in Tuskegee, Alabama, leaving his friends and political allies to fear the worst. Communists planned their protest at Lake Anna Park and demanded the police be investigated.

Barberton townspeople, armed and deputized by their mayor, fought with spectators and Communist Party members during an unauthorized speech at Lake Anna Park. *Barberton Public Library.*

Barberton mayor Seney Decker told newspapers that he had denied a request by two Communist Party subgroups, the International Labor Defense and the League of Struggle for Negro Rights. Speakers scheduled to appear were the party's editor/labor organizer J. Louis Engdahl and Nina Wilcox, of Cleveland, the mother of one of nine African American teenagers facing the electric chair for alleged rape of two white women in Scottsboro, Alabama. Decker said the speakers would cause trouble and had already promised violence in fliers promoting the event. The Communist groups vowed to show up anyway.

There were clues that Decker would draw such a broad line in the sand. Though he denied it later, he had a clear track record of vehement opposition to Communist ideals. Around the time of Alexander's disappearance, Decker told a crowd that included reporters that he

Barberton mayor Seney Decker.
Barberton Public Library.

would "break the…heads of communists" if they came to his city. For a man with his views, there must have been a lot of unfortunate symbolism in the choice of Lake Anna as a site for a speech by disaffected workers. How would it look if hundreds of unemployed men gathered at the center of his town, a company town if there ever was one, founded by überindustrialist O.C. Barber, in the very park Barber named for his daughter? The park also was a literal stone's throw from Decker's office window at city hall and a short walk from a police department that would be quickly overwhelmed if trouble came.

Worrying that his city might not be up to controlling a large, angry crowd wasn't an unreasonable fear. In Decker's lifetime, there was the collective memory of the angry mob that destroyed Akron's city hall in 1900. Whatever his reasons, the mayor conceived a disastrous plan for Barberton that amounted to city-sanctioned vigilante violence. The day of the speech, Decker deputized a small army of "special officers" who attacked visiting Communists, reporters and innocent bystanders with clubs and tear gas.

"In those days it wasn't uncommon for police departments to have a barrel filled with bats and axe handles stashed somewhere," Barberton historian Steve Kelleher said. "In Barberton, they pretty much deputized a whole mob of men who grabbed the clubs and ran across the street to knock some heads."

Plus, Decker denied a permit to the Communist groups nearly a month before the date of the speech—plenty of time for both sides to plan. Not surprisingly, Lake Anna was packed on June 26. Pro- and anti-Communist factions, the mayor's posse, Barberton police and reporters and photographers from three local newspapers faced one another in the park, all waiting to see what would happen next.

"No less than 3,000 were jammed on the strip of ground between the lake and the street," the *Beacon Journal* reported. The word went up: "Here they come," growing in sound until it resembled a roar.

Waves of Decker's special deputies moved through the crowd armed with bats, clubs and tear gas guns. Speakers and their supporters were targeted by the specials as they tried to get to a podium on the bandstand to speak. Witnesses said Barberton police stood by as the beatings

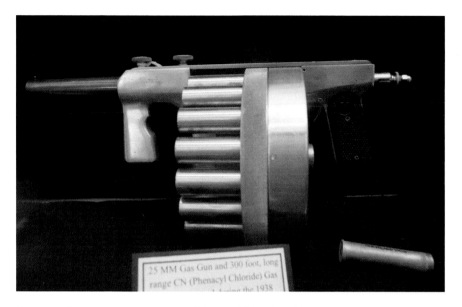

Example of a 25 mm tear gas gun used in the 1930s. *Akron Police Museum, photo by Mike Cardew.*

occurred and the tear gas spread. Many watched from the porch of the Elks Club across the street. At one point, white noxious smoke so filled the air in the park that occupants in houses around the lake either fled or were sickened by the fumes. An unidentified man who tried to talk about the missing African American labor leader was dragged into an alley by city hall and taunted with threats of lynching.

Decker's specials had two basic marching orders: make sure no one gets to speak, and stop anyone from making a record of the violence. A fair amount of blood was spilled to carry out the mayor's orders.

Jack Reed, an editorial writer from the *Akron Times Press*, said that he was roughed up and thrown out of the Barberton Police Department as the specials prepared to go to the park armed with clubs wrapped in newspaper.

Beacon Journal photographer Frank Demshaw and reporter Ed Cunningham were severely beaten trying to take pictures of another group of specials as they shot tear gas at one of the speakers. Demshaw tried twice to set up his camera to shoot the woman, who moved across the park trying to speak between tear gas explosions. On the third attempt, witnesses said Demshaw was clubbed from behind by a two-hundred-pound man who struck him on the head and shoulder. When the photographer fell, others joined in. He was beaten unconscious by the group, who, witnesses said, struck the photographer in the knees and temple.

A bystander who feared Demshaw would be killed by the blows ran twenty-five feet to where two Barberton motorcycle officers were watching from their bikes. The man told the *Beacon Journal* that police shrugged and told him, "Well, you get to take chances. He's got no business with a camera here."

Demshaw regained consciousness sometime later and staggered through the crowd looking for Cunningham, the reporter who was struck down because he had volunteered to hold and fire the camera's flash. Demshaw was eventually spotted injured in the park by Decker, who ordered the photographer be patched up and taken to the mayor's home. A twenty-five-year-old law office employee named W.B. Laurentzen was beaten by specials when he tried to retrieve Demshaw's damaged camera.

Witnesses said that Demshaw and Cunningham identified themselves as members of the press, which seemed to incite the attack. Laurentzen was a bystander who didn't know either man. He was clubbed because he tried to help someone else. Two alleged Communists were hurt the same way.

When Decker's war on Communists spilled over to the press, it sparked an unusual collaboration between normally competitive newspapers. Pictures from the *Akron Times Press* were shared with the *Beacon Journal* and newspapers in Cleveland for the next day's full-page coverage. Colleagues of the injured reporters followed the story in the days after the attack. Many of the mayor's specials turned out to be volunteers from the local American Legion and the nearby branch of the state militia.

None of the special officers was arrested that day. Two Barberton specials were arrested later as a result of a grand jury investigation, as were two Barberton police officers. The officers were convicted of beating C. Louis Alexander after the labor leader returned to Akron and identified them from a group of more than forty men. The two local men who identified themselves as Communists were convicted on felony and misdemeanor assault charges, respectively.

A leader of the specials gave an interesting account of his role during a court appearance reported by the *Beacon Journal*. John Theising, a past American Legion commander, said that Mayor Decker put him in charge of one of two groups of the special officers. He said the mayor ordered him to fire the tear gas at the sign of the first speaker at the podium (the commander of the other specials group denied this). In the days before the riot, Theising said that Decker asked the American Legion drum corps to postpone a planned rehearsal so the group would be free to play, ostensibly to drown out the speakers. He assured the Legion that any damage to their instruments would be paid for, but the group declined.

Tear gas was distributed by police, Theising testified, but not the clubs. The sticks were stored on the front porch of the Elks Club, Theising said. Barberton police chief Fred Werntz testified earlier that he and other officers had indeed gathered there but gave a different account. "Everybody seemed to be having a good time," the chief said in his testimony.

Mayor Decker refused to give the grand jury a list of names of the special officers. The number of officers he deputized fluctuated from more than fifty to "a handful," depending on whether Decker was boasting of his city's might or defending his behavior.

A special named Harry "Jack" White was identified as the man who beat Frank Demshaw. White denied it, but the grand jury indicted him on assault and battery and impersonating an officer. White's lawyer posed an interesting defense of White's actions. He said the photographer and his assistant provoked the attack because the flash gun the men used resembled a revolver—a revolver that took two hands to hold upright and required lighting with a match. In the end, White was fined fifty dollars and sentenced to thirty days in jail.

Back in Barberton, church and city leaders lobbied for Decker's recall for office, but the mayor served out the remainder of his second term unscathed. A park named for Decker still sits at the edge of town near the new middle school.

There is no mention of the riot at Lake Anna Park, nor an account of the riot, in the city's official history.

THE PRETTY BOY
WHO GOT AWAY

Even during the Great Depression, Frank Mitchell looked like a man who had found some success. His neighbors remembered him as a sharp dresser who wore knife-edge pleats in his trousers and double-breasted jackets with fat lapels. His shiny, dark hair was always slicked off his forehead to make him look older, but his round cheeks and open face had just the opposite effect. Though he hated it, folks often described him as a pretty boy.

Mitchell's neighbors at 731 Lodi Street in Goodyear Heights would later say that no one knew that he and his roommates, known in Akron as Nathan King, Bert Walker and housekeeper Nellie Maxwell, were wanted criminals living under a string of aliases. Had they known Mitchell's real name, Charles Arthur "Pretty Boy" Floyd, he would have been recognized immediately.

Floyd's criminal career began in 1922, when he was caught stealing pennies from a post office; three years later, he was convicted of a payroll robbery. The crime bought him five years in prison. Floyd treated his incarceration as a kind of outlaw college. Inside, old-timers taught him to be a more effective bank robber and a craftier fugitive. After his release, he was suspected of several murders, but Floyd's boyish charm and hard-luck upbringing made him a kind of folk hero to many in the grip of the Depression.

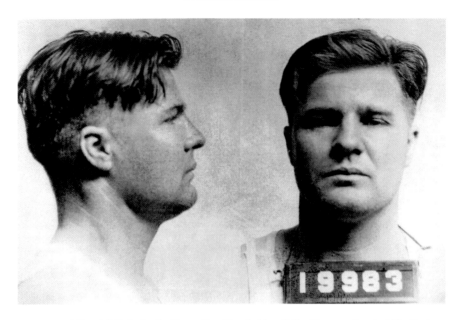

Mug shot of Frank Mitchell, aka Pretty Boy Floyd. *Akron Police Museum, photo by Mike Cardew.*

As Mitchell, Floyd was well liked by his neighbors. William Gannon became his landlord and his friend. Mitchell was a good egg, Gannon believed, at least at first. "I guess he was bad all the time, but was able to conceal it, at least to some of us, for a while," Gannon told a reporter four years after Floyd was last seen in Akron.

It would be some time before Floyd's identity was known in Akron, even though police had him in custody at the Summit County Jail for more than a month in connection with the death of an Akron police officer.

In law enforcement, it was a time before computerized fingerprint searches and DNA, and on Lodi Street, Floyd and his gang faced little of the normal new-neighbor curiosity. Few people stuck their noses into a stranger's business. After all, everyone had his own story. Plus, Floyd had built up some goodwill on the street as Mitchell. He even paid a fine to get Gannon's wife, Bertha, out of jail. While it was true that he and his roommates seemed to come and go a lot, when they returned from wherever they had gone, Floyd and his friends always seemed to be flush and looking for fun.

Where Floyd, fellow gang members and Gannon often went to find fun was just a short drive across town. Second only to North Howard Street in North Hill, an underground economy flourished on Kenmore Boulevard at night. The pulled shades and closed doors of many of the houses concealed after-hours establishments wryly called "resorts," where visitors could buy a game, a drink or companionship of a temporary sort. Every now and then the vice squad would make a big show of closing down a hot spot, but another would appear almost the next day. The greater Akron area faced 60 percent industrial unemployment in 1930, so as long as everyone maintained some level of decorum, the money illegal businesses brought to the local economy was a relative good that outweighed the bad in tough economic times.

Whatever agreement existed between police and the people of Kenmore's mini Reeperbahn, it all ended at 1:30 a.m. on Saturday, March 8, when a beat cop named Harland F. Manes was shot after a minor traffic stop.

According to press and police records, two vice cops were on the street investigating a house of ill repute when they saw a pair of women staggering out of the house toward a parked car. The women said they intended to join their companions, and one of them pointed out the car at the corner, where Floyd gang mates Bert Walker and Nathan King were waiting.

At this point, every member of the gang was wanted for a robbery at Farmers & Merchants Bank and several other crimes in northwest Ohio. Perhaps Walker worried they'd be found out if questioned or their Akron hideout would be discovered, so as soon as the women were in the car, he raced away from the curb and struck another vehicle during a hasty U-turn. Suddenly, Officer Manes was at Walker's side of the stalled car as one of the vice cops grabbed King from the passenger's side and dragged him to the patrol car. Walker opened fire, striking Manes in the stomach at close range. As the officer lay mortally wounded in the street, police shot after Walker. He was hit but managed to flee in the confusion, as did both women.

Within the hour, every available Akron officer converged on Kenmore Boulevard looking for Walker and the missing women, while Manes clung to life in People's Hospital under heavy guard. King was in custody but wasn't talking. Finally, police got a break—one of the women was identified as Bertha Gannon. In a search of her home, investigators found what they were looking for: a phone number on the wall that would lead them to Walker and, by default, to Floyd.

Detective Eddie McDonnell led eight city policemen considered to be the best shooters on the force in a raid on the Lodi Street house. The men wore bulletproof vests and charged up the steps behind McDonnell into the yellow two-story house the gang used as its hideout. McDonnell came face to face with Maxwell inside the door. Without a word, she pointed him to a flight of stairs leading to the second floor.

According to the *Beacon Journal*, Walker was discovered in a bedroom, lying on a blood-soaked sheet. The cover hid his injuries—a gunshot wound in each arm—and a machine gun clip with 150 rounds.

Hearing a noise under the bed, McDonnell ordered, "Blow his head off if he doesn't come out."

Floyd was dragged from beneath the bed by one leg while shouting, "I didn't shoot anyone!"

A search of the rest of the house revealed a gang preparing for fight or flight. Packed suitcases stood ready on the second floor. Inside the house was a cache of arms the *Beacon Journal* described as one of the most complete arsenals in the state. "Rifles, revolvers and shotguns were distributed advantageously throughout the house, where they would be handy in event of a siege with police, were confiscated. A [bag] was filled with revolvers, a small quantity of nitroglycerin and rubber gloves…all the paraphernalia of the modern-day gangster and gunman."

Two stolen automobiles and car license plates from Ohio, Michigan and Indiana also were found by police. The Studebaker that Walker drove the night of the shooting had a niche cut out of its back window wide enough for the muzzle of a tommy gun to poke through for rolling shootouts.

Walker and Floyd were taken to Manes's room at People's Hospital, where the officer identified Walker as his assailant. Manes died a few hours later surrounded by his fellow officers. Walker was being treated down the hall under heavy guard.

Walker was charged with Manes's murder while recovering. Maxwell, King and Floyd were jailed as material witnesses and charged with

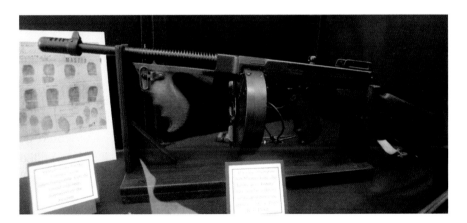

Guns recovered in the arrest of Floyd and his gang. *Akron Police Museum, photo by Mike Cardew.*

harboring a fugitive. All four were booked under their aliases, Floyd as Frank Mitchell, aka Pretty Boy Smith.

The future Public Enemy Number One made good use of his time in Summit's jail. Portraying himself to investigators as a young man (nineteen, rather than his true age of twenty-six) who fell under the influence of more experienced middle-aged criminals, Floyd managed to hide his criminal background from captors and, it's said, even managed to charm a few.

The masquerade wasn't to last, however. News of the shootout generated interest in the gang from police around the state as well as Chicago, Kansas City and New York. Finally, officers from Toledo identified Mitchell as Floyd. He and Nathan King were taken to Lucas County, where the two were charged with the February robbery of Farmers & Merchants Bank. On May 20, they each were sentenced to twelve to fifteen years in the Ohio Penitentiary for armed robbery.

Walker was convicted of Manes's murder and sentenced to death under his assumed name (only his attorney knew his true identity, the purported son of a monied Texas family). During his trial and appeals, he continued to taunt McDonnell about Floyd. "You haven't heard the last of that Mitchell boy."

After his conviction in Toledo, Floyd vowed that he'd rather die than go back to the pen. Handcuffed to King for the train ride to the Ohio Penitentiary, he was good on his word. Seconds after the train left its last stop, Floyd somehow managed to break a bathroom window and jump from the moving train. Police heard the crash and ran to the back of the train to find King standing by a toilet and a broken window. The

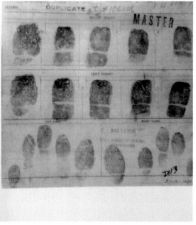

The booking card for Floyd lists his name as Frank Mitchell, the alias by which he was known for much of his time in Akron. *Akron Police Museum, photo by Mike Cardew.*

handcuffs that had bound Floyd to him hung from his wrist. Once again, King wasn't ratting on a friend. Police suspect that Floyd obtained a key to the handcuffs and smuggled it out hidden under his tongue.

Pretty Boy Floyd made his escape fewer than ten miles from the door of his intended prison cell. He would live another four years, to the frustration of police, traveling in and out of Akron and Youngstown. On October 22, Floyd was shot to death in East Liverpool, Ohio, while trying to escape from FBI agents.

Interestingly, the sale of Floyd's arsenal to the FBI museum provided funds to arm Akron's first SWAT team, according to Akron Police Museum historian James Conley.

Now, eighty years later, the Pretty Boy who got away remains the subject of an ongoing Akron police investigation. Floyd's booking sheets and other information the department kept out of the sale to the FBI disappeared about a decade ago. Modern-day detectives recently tracked down some of the items for sale on the Internet.

PART III

VILLAINS AND ROGUES, ACTS OF GOD, FOLLY OF MEN

Akron bounced back as a major industrial city after the Great Depression, thanks to the rubber companies that manufactured supplies needed to serve three wars over four decades. The men who left here to fight returned home to the plants and to their neighborhoods. By the 1950s, the air was thick with soot from the thriving factories, the city and its suburbs were packed, shopping malls were going up seemingly overnight and the schools were overflowing.

Akron was reborn.

Unions for rubber, steel and autoworkers gave Rubber City kids a choice for the very first time: leave school for the factories of your fathers and a middle-class job for life or go to college and become what your parents never dreamed.

Before the Rust Belt cast its pall over Akron, entrepreneurs also flourished here. While some moved from the wrong to the right side of the law, others found their promise mired by feet of clay. Like everywhere, there were triumphs and tragedies, spectacular success stories and stunning failures.

WHISKEY DICK

Liborio Percoco was larger than life in every way that mattered. The man who was known to everyone but his wife and mother as "Whiskey Dick" achieved the American Dream on both sides of the law, first as the city's best-known bootlegger and later as an indefatigable millionaire bail bondsman.

In his prime, "Whiskey Dick" was 290 pounds of ambition, nerve and connections, stuffed into his trademark trench coat like *cotechino* topped with a handmade felt fedora. Percoco loved opera, his local notoriety and his girth—proof positive that he was no longer the skinny kid from southern Italy who came here in steerage on a ship bound for New York. He was fourteen at the time of the voyage. Percoco liked to tell the story of arriving in America without shoes—someone stole his pair while he slept on a straw mat in the belly of the boat. It was likely one of the last times he went without.

North Hill was both haven and ghetto when Percoco came to Akron from Newark, Ohio, to marry in 1917. The young husband was well settled into his factory job by 1920 when Prohibition came. That year, however, the family lost its house to fire, and Percoco needed a second job. In the search, he found the opportunity that would change the course of his life.

Most nights, Percoco finished his factory job and headed for a local restaurant, where he would wait tables for tips— sometimes less than a

Artist's caricature of Liborio "Whiskey Dick" Percoco. *Akron* Beacon Journal.

dollar a night. It didn't take long for him to notice that the real action was going on in the backroom, which operated as a speakeasy. Almost immediately, Percoco went from running illegal booze to making it. In time, he had saved enough money to give up the factory job and open a small store. The North Valley Grocery functioned mainly as a front for the whiskey that Percoco would sell out the back door by the bucket and to roadhouses in Portage Lakes, Copley and as far away as Portage County. At his peak, Percoco ran the largest still in Summit County, rumored to hold five hundred gallons at a time.

Years later, he loved to give out his special recipe for whiskey, a homemade blend that he boasted never caused anyone to go blind. Here's Percoco's recipe, as told to the *Beacon Journal*. You'll need a barrel and a still.

You take a 50-gallon wood barrel, and you put in one sack of lump corn sugar. It costs about $2. You put in five pounds of corn meal and six pounds of cake yeast and fill it with water to about five inches from the top. It should start fermenting. After you ferment it, then you use your still. You put in the mash by the bucket. You have a fire under the pot, and when it starts boiling, the fumes go in this tube where it's cooled and the whiskey comes out the end. The first batch is 188-proof alcohol. You cut it with water. Never had any problem. They drank it and got drunk. That's what it was for.

Percoco never really forgot being the hungry, shoeless kid who worked with his dad in an Italian factory when he was only ten years old. Legend has it that he left out whiskey and bologna and crackers at his store for the newspaper delivery boys, reporters and police. The gesture brought Percoco much goodwill and a practical immunity from prosecution—for a while.

Then, about 1922, Whiskey Dick got the nickname that made him wealthy and made him an unavoidable target of law enforcement. As the story goes, a local reporter tried to blackmail Percoco by threatening him with a story that outed him as a bootlegger king who controlled the city. Whether the shakedown actually took place, the *Akron Evening Times* carried this headline: "Whiskey Dick Rules Akron."

It turned out to be the best advertising a small businessman could hope for. Customers from outside North Hill flooded the neighborhood to do business with the famous Whiskey Dick.

Unfortunately for Percoco, between 1926 and 1930 police also took notice in a more official way. Sometimes the notoriety worked to his advantage. Percoco was so well liked by police that when rival bootleggers started shooting one another, he could count on being jailed—not because he was a suspect but because no one wanted the colorful con to be the next dead bootlegger.

With Whiskey Dick becoming more well known outside his neighborhood, life continued to become more and more complicated for Percoco. The cost of doing business got bigger: suddenly there were local, county and state liquor agents to "befriend." Still, it was business as

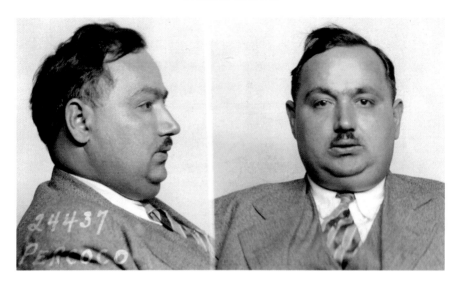

Percoco's mug shot. *Akron* Beacon Journal.

usual for the most part—several arrests, no convictions. The ride ended in the fall of 1931, when Percoco and twenty-four others were arrested by federal agents who crowed that a "liquor mob" that had supplied illegal booze from Akron to Columbus for two years had been smashed. Seized in the arrest, according to a police report, were "740 gallons of liquor and a perfectly good automobile." The initial tip for the federal arrests was credited to Akron police.

When Percoco was sentenced to twenty-two months in a federal lockup in Pennsylvania in 1932, it seemed that Whiskey Dick was finished—but the penalty proved to be another stroke of odd good luck. Since Percoco had handled meat in his grocery store, a friendly fellow inmate got him a job as the prison butcher. Percoco ended up supervising ten men, learned to type, sang in the prison choir and eliminated theft in the kitchen. In return, he did his time in a cell with a private shower. In nine months, Percoco was free on the glowing recommendation of his warden.

Whiskey Dick wasn't exactly finished with the illegal liquor business upon his release. He and others took advantage of the short time after the end of Prohibition when state stores did not yet exist. Percoco reportedly made a brief good living getting liquor to restaurants that now had every legal right to sell it. Percoco also dabbled in running numbers but found it less lucrative than alcohol. In 1934, he financed a nightclub called the Ritz, which Percoco described as the finest gin joint between Chicago and New York. The bar did phenomenally well, making more than $8,000 in its first week of business, but Percoco's career as a club owner would be short-lived.

State liquor agents—who Percoco always said hated to see an ex-con make money—suspended the Ritz liquor license for selling rum on Sundays. A few weeks later, one of the same agents accused Percoco of selling him illegal whiskey from his grocery in a particularly novel way. The agent said a clerk ran the liquor to his car while he parked in front of Percoco's grocery store. A judge dismissed the "curb service" charge when Percoco produced two witnesses in his favor and the agent produced none.

Around that time, Percoco started looking for a way to make money that was a little further off police radar. Since his bootlegger buddies were still getting arrested, Percoco got the idea to use his home and store as collateral to bail out his friends. Risky, but as long as there was honor among bootleggers…and thieves…and prostitutes…Percoco made a profit on the loans when the cases were settled. Soon his phone was ringing a dozen times a day, and Whiskey Dick had a new career as a bail bondsman. He often joked that the transition was natural because he already knew all the cops and the criminals.

That knowledge, coupled with the financial stake of a friend who also made money in the bootlegging business, was the beginning of Percoco's business, P&C Bonding. Over four decades, P&C became the largest bonding operation in the country. Percoco hired ex-cops and marines to staff offices in thirty-eight states and paid rewards to jilted wives, scorned lovers and former co-workers who led him to anyone foolish enough to skip bail. Percoco made his own wanted posters and was said to have a network of friendly law enforcement sources across the United States and Canada. In Akron, seven P&C agents were on call twenty-four hours a day. It was common for those accused to meet up with one of Percoco's representatives at the Summit County Jail before their fingerprint ink had dried. Percoco's company posted bond for more than one thousand defendants each week during its heyday.

Percoco in his office at P&C bonding holding a wanted poster. *Akron* Beacon Journal.

In those days, people who couldn't raise enough money on their own would hire a bondsman to make bail. The bonding company paid the entire amount against a 10 percent payment from the arrested person and collateral for the rest—often money, jewelry or deeds to property owned by relatives and friends. If the person showed up for court, the bondsman kept the down payment and returned the balance, making a profit on each bond. If not, the bondsman was stuck for the full amount.

Whiskey Dick rarely got stuck. He quickly gained a reputation as someone you didn't want to leave holding the bag. A favorite story in the Summit County courts goes like this: Percoco once paid a fireman ten dollars to park in front of the courthouse. The wanted man Percoco bonded had died in a fire. All the proof the judge needed was visible, deceased and sizzling in the bed of the fire truck when the judge looked out his window…and Whiskey Dick received his refund.

Percoco once nabbed a client as he stepped off a plane in Italy. The fact that both men were in the same airport a world away from Akron was just another stroke of friendly fate for the bondsman.

Occasionally, Percoco would put up his own money for bond as a matter of principle. That was the case with striking steel workers in Youngstown and Mansfield. Some months later, Percoco received a call from one of the men he had bailed out from the picket line of another strike. "I know a guy you're looking for," the caller said. "He's working at our factory. Come and get the scab."

Among the most famous fleeing felons was Jimmy Hoffa, for whom Percoco put up $150,000 from his Chicago office.

Percoco vowed to spend his last dime to bring Frank Hurn back to Akron. Hurn fleeced Akron investors of more than $100,000 on the promise of bringing a minor league football team to town. When Hurn was found in Miami with children clinging to each leg, Percoco admitted to a moment of sympathy. Nonetheless, Hurn was returned to Akron by the Summit County Sheriff's Department—thanks to a tip from a P&C contact.

The grandson of an Akron pawnshop owner, John Jones, remembers hearing stories about Percoco's drive to get his man. Bob Philpot of Garrettsville remembered:

> *In the fifties, my grandfather was a mechanic at Firestone. He also owned Johnny's Swap Shop. The shop was a hangout for all sorts of politicians, police union officers and anyone who walked through the door with something to sell. I am sure a few pieces of hot merchandise would occasionally be traded at Johnny's, and most certainly, the daily numbers were run from there.*
>
> *You would always hear the men talking, "Percoco got him out of jail." I always assumed that this fellow was some kind of lawyer who helped my grandfather. My grandmother used to say, "How ironic is it that John was arrested for selling numbers for the same guy who pulled strings to get him out of it?"*

Philpot's grandfather later became a Summit County deputy and remained close to Percoco. Sometime later, Jones asked for Percoco's help when the husband of a family member was arrested. The bond was made, and then the man vanished. According to Philpot family lore, Jones told Whiskey Dick where to find his absent relative. Whiskey Dick drove to Murphy, North Carolina, and found his fugitive. "After an altercation, Whiskey Dick subdued him with a blackjack and stuffed him into the trunk of his car," Philpot said. "With no interstate highways back then, I am sure the ride back to Akron was over twenty-four hours."

Percoco's career hit a minor bump in 1961 when it was discovered that he had taken answers from a subordinate on an insurance licensing exam and had twice declined to disclose his 1932 federal conviction to state insurance regulators.

Despite a small mountain of reference letters from local judges, attorneys and politicians, the state suspended Percoco's bonding license, which made it impossible for P&C to insure the money spent by the company on its bonds. The decision hardly put a dent in Percoco's business plan. He simply used his own assets to guarantee his expense. That's the way P&C did business until the state reinstated Percoco's license in 1963.

In the mid-1970s, a change in state law effectively eliminated the need for commercial bonding agents. Percoco continued to go to his tiny downtown office in the Second National Bank Building long after there was any business or financial need. Folks said he had more than enough money to stay home, but he didn't like to be there once his wife, Francesca, moved to a nearby rest home.

Percoco died in 1980 at age eighty-three. In forty-two years in business, only forty-seven people got away from Whiskey Dick.

BILL GRIFFITHS

For the better part of forty years, the man who was likely Barberton's most successful criminal also was one of the city's biggest benefactors. From the 1920s through the early '60s, Bill Griffiths didn't even try to hide.

Griffiths got his start in his father "Pop" Griffiths's storefront pool hall/cigar store on Wooster Avenue. By the time he was twenty, the younger Griffiths had taken over the family business and moved it to the Meehan Building, a large former bottling plant less than a block from city hall. Renamed Griffiths Sports Shop, the new location offered outsiders a game of pool or cards and drinks and sandwiches from the lunch counter on the large first floor. Insiders—which included virtually everyone—knew that Griffiths's real business thrived behind a false wall.

From that not-so secret room, Griffiths took a piece of virtually every gaming activity going on in Summit County: punchboards, poker and dice games, fifty-cent baseball tickets, two-dollar horse bets—even the occasional traveling carnival.

The business was worth millions—which would have been a trick if Griffiths's income only came from backroom gambling. It didn't. He did two other things near perfectly. To begin with, he reportedly was one of the largest suppliers of layoff bets in the Midwest. Here's how the layoff worked: Griffiths would accept large single bets by telephone from

Bill Griffiths (front row, bow tie) and "Pops" Griffiths (in suspenders) in front of their pool hall, circa 1915. *Barberton Public Library.*

Punchboards taken in a gambling raid. *Akron Police Museum, photo by Mike Cardew.*

bookies all over the country. Those bookies made big wagers to cover the amount their customers bet with them. Imagine that the bookie's customers bet virtually unanimously that the Yankees would win the World Series. If the Yankees won, that bookie took a huge financial hit. Layoff bets were a kind of insurance policy against the customers being right. In the example, our bookie made enough money with his side bet to cover what he would have lost to his customers because he had a huge payday coming from Griffiths—allegedly. That's a layoff. As the house, the advantage for Griffith was obvious—he earned a cut of every layoff bet placed with him, win or lose.

Griffiths also knew a trend when he saw one. He and a group of investors bought Ascot racetrack in Northampton for back taxes about the time parimutuel betting was legalized in Ohio. For the next twenty years, he had a piece of the action on both sides of the track.

Unidentified boy at Ascot Park. Griffiths owned the local racetrack through the early 1950s. *Photo by Ott Gangl.*

Even though the success of his bookie joint was an open secret, no one dared make a run for the gambling king's money. Griffiths was notoriously security minded. Old-timers always swore he paid a man with a tommy gun to stand guard on the third floor of the Sports Shop through most of the '20s and '30s. Griffiths's outwardly unassuming home was built with heavy brick walls because he feared a rival might want to burn it down. Windows were made of triple-thick glass, just in case someone else had a tommy gun. The house also was one of only three in Barberton to have an elevator. Griffiths used his elevator because he had trouble walking and climbing after contracting polio as a teenager. As an adult, he was known to conduct much of his business at the Sports Shop from a tall leather chair that is now owned by the Barberton Historical Society.

The minifortress of a house and a lifelong love of cockfighting were just about Griffiths's only conspicuous expenses. He raised his own birds and traveled around the country to watch them fight. When more traditional transport from a cockfight in Florida wasn't available (thanks

The Meehan Building in Barberton, where Griffiths Sports Shop was located. Griffiths supposedly kept a guard with a tommy gun posted on the third floor. *Barberton Public Library.*

to a hurricane), Griffiths hailed a cab and headed for Ohio. The meter ran all the way home.

There was one other way Griffiths was known to spend freely—story after story paints him as the town's own version of a gambler Robin Hood.

At the height of the Depression, Griffiths paid off the mortgage on the local Elks Lodge to save the club from foreclosure. Fairly often during that time, men who were lucky enough to be working lost their entire week's pay at Sports Shop craps tables. A wife with the courage to complain would occasionally get back the money—along with her husband. The misbehaving spouse usually was delivered to her by the scruff of the neck with a gruff warning from Griffiths: "I better not see either of you two again."

Gifts of everything from new band uniforms to police cruisers appeared in Barberton, courtesy of Griffiths. A profile in the *Barberton Herald* written decades after his death described him regularly shelling out payments to local charities by peeling fifties from a fat roll of bills, asking, "How much do I owe this year?"

There were no vice forfeiture laws at the time—cities couldn't legally keep valuable illegally earned assets—so Griffiths's local largesse probably was a big factor in his run of good fortune with police. Also, his business— though reputedly the largest of its kind in Summit County—wasn't anywhere near rare. Back then, Barberton was packed with competing gambling operators. Newspapers and police reports show that many were regularly rousted, often at the point of an axe...except Griffiths.

For decades, authorities coexisted with the self-made mogul in their midst—as time passed, to the growing ire of his rivals and a smattering of politicians. By the late '40s, arrests were made at the Sports Shop on a regular basis—and just as often everyone but Griffiths faced a legal penalty. A handful of court cases were filed and argued that accused Griffiths of defrauding customers through gambling at the Sports Shop. One claimed a loss of $300,000. Even the Kefauver Senate Hearings on organized crime mentioned Griffiths's gambling business in its investigation of northeast Ohio. Luckily for Griffiths, his operation paled next to Cleveland heavyweights with Vegas connections like Moe Dalitz and the Mayfield Road Gang. When the Internal Revenue Service started asking questions, Griffiths simply applied for a federal tax stamp and started paying 10 percent on his gambling earnings—or at least 10 percent of the income the government could verify. That was the last he heard from the feds.

Gambling was still illegal locally, but when reporters came calling, Griffiths's son Jack explained candidly what father and son planned to do with the federal license. "Gambling," he told the *Beacon Journal*, "every kind of gambling." The following day, the Sports Shop was open for business.

Barberton mayor Catherine Dobbs accused police and the prosecutor of being in cahoots with the gambler down the street. Criminals complained of favoritism. Newspaper editorials asked whether only the governor or attorney general had the will to close down Griffiths's operation. The answer was always the same: "He operates on the quiet," police said. "When we have the evidence, we'll arrest him."

On a chilly November night in 1957, a man named Nelson Glessner took authorities at their word. As the story goes, Glessner wasn't just after money: he apparently was after proof that would put his biggest competition out of business. Police found the remnants of a robbery

Seized tally sheets for sports wagering and layoff bets. *Akron Police Museum, photo by Mike Cardew.*

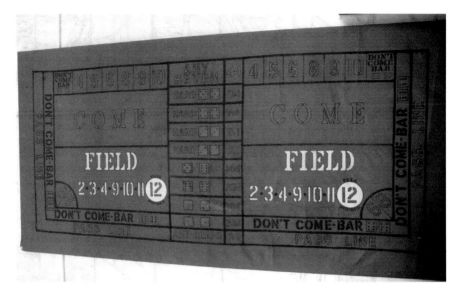

Mat used for illegal dice games. *Akron Police Museum, photo by Mike Cardew.*

all over the Sports Shop parking lot. Griffiths's office file cabinet was upended outside the building. Reams of parlay sheets, contact numbers and betting tickets blew down Tuscarawas Avenue toward police who had previously ignored Griffiths.

Unfortunately for Glessner, police also found him. He was jailed immediately and charged with possession of gambling devices. A fine of $1,000 and six-month jail sentence eventually were reduced to a $100 fine.

Interestingly, police seized enough evidence in the Glessner robbery to finally put the Sports Shop out of business, but the evidence was returned to Griffiths the next day. Why? Because Griffiths called the chief and asked him to give back his personal property. The chief complied, even though Griffiths's request was tantamount to an admission of guilt.

The following day, the Sports Shop was open for business.

The city solicitor, equivalent to Barberton's current law director, initially was slow to investigate Griffiths. The police chief, after all, had been instructed by a city judge to keep only what was necessary to prosecute Glessner and return the rest, and it wasn't clear whether the chief would even sign Griffiths's arrest warrant.

Barberton's mayor kept complaining to anyone who would listen—including the Summit County prosecutor—that the police and possibly the city's legal department had mishandled evidence. At first, few people paid attention. The female chief executive regularly operated outside the Barberton boys' club and was seen as a bit of a killjoy in her criticism of Griffiths, much like her previous crusade to eliminate "girlie" magazines from the shelves of local stores.

What city administrators weren't as willing to dismiss was their growing reputation as a county embarrassment. A letter to Mayor Dobbs from County Prosecutor John S. Ballard scolded the city. "It appears evident that gambling has been going on here for some time, as the evidence given to [the solicitor] could not have sprung up overnight. It is somewhat a puzzle why only Glessner was charged and Griffiths ignored."

Pressured by Ballard, Barberton got a court order to disconnect phone lines to the Sports Shop and made regular, if fruitless, patrols. By then, Griffiths was in his early sixties, had sold the racetrack at a profit and was concentrating on his legitimate businesses, a local swim club and the Loyal Oak Golf Course in the town next door—which, according to local historians, had its betting wire disconnected years before the Sports Shop robbery.

According to Mayor Dobbs's own letter to her prosecutor, Griffiths ended up with the last laugh. "I have in file a police report that on each shift a policeman has checked this Sports Shop daily, on each of three shifts, and has turned up nothing."

The letter was dated November 17, 1958. Almost a year after the robbery, the Sports Shop remained open, and Griffiths was doing business on his own terms.

THE DOODLEBUG

A double head-on rail collision on a summer night in 1940 is Summit County's deadliest crash. At about 6:00 p.m. on July 31, people in Cuyahoga Falls reported hearing a deafening explosion and then a loud rumble. Wood on the houses near the Front Street and Bailey Road junction of the Pennsylvania Railroad was blackened by the smoke from the fire. Drivers within a mile of the intersections had to close their car windows against waves of heat. Witnesses close enough to see the trains reported a gruesome sight: a single car gas commuter line locals called the Doodlebug had somehow missed its switch-off point and smashed into an oncoming seventy-three-car, 250-ton freight train.

Onlookers said the Doodlebug folded like tissue paper. The larger train had hit it so hard that it wrapped around the smaller one and pushed the Doodlebug two hundred yards backward along the tracks. Flames fueled by the Doodlebug's 350-gallon gas tank shot into the air and licked around the car, trapping forty-three passengers inside. Investigators would later say nine people died on impact, and thirty-four were burned beyond recognition. Some would die piled atop fellow passengers, arms and legs akimbo in a futile rush to escape the blaze and smoke through the Doodlebug's windows. The flaming fuel that spilled along the train tracks also set the freight cars ablaze.

A fireman (far left) is barely visible through the smoke as he clears the Doodlebug of baggage and bodies. *Akron–Summit County Public Library.*

Most of the passengers on the Doodlebug were regular commuters from jobs in Cleveland. Some had family members waiting to meet them after a day's work. As news of the crash spread, thousands flocked to the tracks to try to help or just stare in astonishment.

Cuyahoga Falls sent every fire engine, ambulance and police vehicle. A call for help was answered by fire departments in Barberton, Kent, Akron and Ravenna. Bodies were taken to three hospital morgues and about a dozen funeral homes throughout the Falls and Akron. Family members traveled to each site, simultaneously hoping for and dreading the sight of their loved ones. Often, identification wasn't possible. Other times the only point of familiarity was a wedding ring, a watch or a pair of shoes. Summit County coroner R.E. Amos said the dead were trapped in a steel car when the gas exploded; the intense heat likely fused shut the windows and doors. By the time the windows snapped from the blaze, anyone who wasn't burned was overcome by smoke.

Jean Hudson recalled the site of the crash for a memory project of the Cuyahoga Falls Historical Society. "When we got there, people were screaming and the smell of burning flesh was overcoming. The air was thick with it. My dad went into the train and said there were body parts everywhere. My little sister remembers a man being thrown to the back of the train with both legs missing."

Another woman wrote that her mother saw a woman who seemed unharmed holding a charred infant in her arms.

At first, tankers from the volunteer fire departments were limited to spraying the crash with water. It was nearly an hour before the heat and flames had subsided enough for crews to begin clearing bodies from the Doodlebug.

Father Joseph Butler, a Catholic priest from Cleveland who was visiting friends in the Falls, walked among the dead and pieces of the dead piled along the tracks, dispensing absolution by the light of rescue flares.

In air filled with smoke and soot, rescuers failed quickly. They were relieved by volunteers from other departments and the unidentified men and women who drove to the crash to offer their help. It was three hours before the last body was removed from the wreckage.

Only three people riding the Doodlebug that day escaped death. Railroad employee Tod Wonn told newspapers that he was riding home in the back of the baggage car when he saw the conductor running toward him yelling, "Jump—we're going to crash!" The Doodlebug's engineer also jumped to safety. Wonn said that his next memory was of rolling down a hill in burning clothes.

The freight train was three hours late on the night of the crash. Its engineer said that he saw the Doodlebug coming around the bend and jammed on the brakes, but the space was too short to stop the trains from smashing together. He and another man jumped from the train through what he described to the *New York Times* as "a wall of flames without knowing what lay beyond."

A report ordered to investigate the crash indicated that the Pennsylvania Railroad installed a motorized signal that might have kept the trains from crashing two months to the day after the Doodlebug missed its stop. The railroad paid out $600,000 to the families of the dead. A replacement Doodlebug was running within a month.

DISORDER IN THE COURT

James V. Barbuto probably always was a man torn between two worlds: the tough one he lived in as a welfare kid on the streets of Akron and the life of privilege he won in Summit County politics. That duality fueled his drive, won him success after success and, it seems likely, was the source of his fatal hubris.

Until it vanished a few years ago, a campaign sign on the wall in a nearby college bar summed up the career of Akron's most infamous judge as well as anything. The entreaty in heavy bold print read "Barbuto for Judge," as if success was a given; a lace bra and panty set hung from one corner of the poster.

Arguably the most popular elected officeholder of his era, Barbuto's nearly two-decade-long political career began as a legal representative for the United Rubber Workers. The self-made lawyer from the rough side of town had a confident swagger and enough natural charisma to turn a deep bench of union brothers and sisters into voters who supported him in races for Summit County prosecutor, common pleas and probate judge races.

The judge's run in elective office unraveled right down the hall from the courtroom where he passed judgment on others. Barbuto faced a twenty-six-count indictment of sexual misconduct that ranged from attempted rape to soliciting prostitution while in office. In addition to the

James V. Barbuto in his chambers at the Summit County Courthouse. *Photo by Ott Gangl.*

sex charges, Barbuto was accused of intimidating investigators and keeping guns for himself that had been seized as evidence.

At his sentencing, Barbuto became the first Ohio jurist in 177 years to be convicted of a felony. And almost every element of the dramatic fall from grace played out in the glare of national television cameras— including allegations that the judge kept a cache of porn in his chambers and liked to dress up in women's underwear and be roughed up by hookers.

A 1980 episode of the ABC news magazine *20/20* titled "Injustice for All" focused on claims that Barbuto handed out reduced sentences to women with whom he had sex and sent an ex-con to intimidate anyone who complained about his behavior. Reporter Geraldo Rivera made his reputation for ambush journalism by chasing supposed henchman William Gordon "Bobie" Brooks through Akron's downtown streets with a cameraman yelling, "Are you Barbuto's hit man?"

Barbuto hired James Burdon to represent him and waived his right to a trial by jury. Burdon was, and is, among the best criminal attorneys money can buy in Summit County. A reformed rough kid himself, Burdon is the son of a union leader and got his first legal job from the judge he would agree to defend.

Despite a number of witnesses and investigations by local police and the Federal Bureau of Investigation, Burdon doesn't think he was fighting a losing battle—even three decades later when the outcome is known. "They didn't get near what they charged him with and I don't think they really proved their convictions…but," Burdon conceded, "if you are going to convict a sitting judge of felonies, the sentence was appropriate."

As shocking as the televised details were, it was just a preview to the daily show that went on during the trial before visiting Judge George J. McMonagle.

A Cleveland bartender named Essie Vaughn Pryor told the court that Barbuto gave her probation on a shooting conviction in return for sex. Another woman described multiple sex acts in Barbuto's chambers. In return, Arinthia Wims testified that she sought Barbuto's help in getting her husband released from jail and obtaining subsidized housing for a friend.

Women who testified to willing and unwilling encounters with Barbuto said that he showed them obscene material. The judge testified that he kept the materials handy for use in antipornography lectures.

Female court employees said they received rewards for sex that included pay raises and the installation of an office air conditioner. One courthouse employee said that Barbuto grabbed her breasts and put his hands up her skirt when she met in his chambers to ask his advice in becoming a court reporter.

The judge had many detractors in court, but he also had friends. Burdon questioned a court secretary who said pay raises were given to everyone and that the air conditioner was part of a courthouse renovation.

The *Pittsburgh Post Gazette* wrote that Barbuto initially denied even knowing the women. When asked if he had had sexual relations in his chambers with anyone other than his wife since 1971, the paper reported that "the judge sighed, put his hand on his forehead and answered, 'Yes.' He was not pressed to identify the partner."

Nearly as sensational as the sexual misdeeds alleged at trial was the depth of Barbuto's influence to network, threaten or schmooze away rumor and suspicion. Two sheriff's deputies testified that they began investigating Barbuto three years earlier after more than one prostitute they arrested told them, "You can't fool with me—I know Barbuto." The inquiry ended when their boss, Sheriff Anthony Cardarelli, ordered it closed after the judge made a personal call.

According to the *Spokane Daily Chronicle*, Judge McMonagle believed the deputies' description of Barbuto's threat. "This is a two way street. If you want to play this game, I can play harder. I have a lot of friends out there."

The courtroom was packed with local and national reporters. The *Boston Globe*, the *New York Times* and *Jet* magazine provided gavel-to-gavel coverage alongside reporters from the *Beacon Journal* and the *Cleveland Plain Dealer*. Initially, though, Akron police detectives Helmut Klemm and Ed Duval didn't have much luck persuading local media to cover the story of a corrupt judge based on the word of witnesses who, in many cases, stood accused in his court. Klemm and Duval sent a letter to *20/20* with the tip about Barbuto that brought Rivera to town for a series of combative interviews and theatrical press conferences.

The FBI got interested when the investigation uncovered that weapons seized as evidence were potentially misappropriated by Barbuto, the sheriff, the coroner and a retired Akron police detective. By then, the momentum was unstoppable, despite resistance from Barbuto's colleagues. Summit County prosecutor Stephen Gabalac initially refused to present the case to a grand jury. He was replaced by special prosecutor Orval Hoover. McMonagle was named visiting judge when Barbuto's colleagues on the Summit Common Pleas Court recused themselves.

After a week-long trial, Barbuto was convicted of only two felonies: one count of gross sexual imposition for the attack on a courthouse employee and one count of intimidation for his dealings with the sheriff's detectives. He pleaded guilty to two misdemeanor charges of dereliction of duty in a separate trial concerning the weapons. The judge also agreed to resign from the court and gave up his right to practice law. Nine of the charges, including an allegation of attempted rape, were tossed out because the time to prosecute them had expired.

Although he was sentenced to one to ten years in prison, Barbuto was released on shock probation after serving seventy-eight days at the Chillicothe Correctional Institution. At the hearing for Barbuto's early release, Burdon said his client was deaf in one ear, suffered from throat cancer and was a suicide risk.

Barbuto's convictions were the first rumbles of an avalanche that buried other powerful Summit County Democrats and toppled the entire structure of local government. In 1979, voters approved a switch to a charter form of government, designed to divide power between a county executive and large elected council rather than concentrate influence in three county commissioners. Sheriff Cardarelli pleaded guilty to three misdemeanors stemming from the weapons allegations and promised never to run for office again. Prosecutor Gabalac was voted out in the next election and opened a private practice in Toledo. A retired police captain and chief coroner's investigator were convicted of dereliction of duty and gun trafficking.

Almost no one involved in the case walked away unscathed. William "Bobie" Brooks, described in the *20/20* program as Barbuto's enforcer and a "street knowledgeable jive turkey," already had a 1970 manslaughter conviction under his belt when he received probation on a charge of obstructing justice for contacting female witnesses on behalf of Barbuto. Brooks was sentenced to prison in 1986 for aggravated assault. He was released in 2001.

Rivera came back to town with his own gang of lawyers to answer a $40 million lawsuit brought by Brooks that he had libeled the ex-con in *20/20*'s tale of sex and corruption. The network won, but Brooks appealed the case for thirteen years, ending when the U.S. Supreme Court finally declined to hear the case.

That wasn't the end of ABC's troubles for its visit to Akron. A woman linked to Barbuto who said Rivera invaded her privacy lost her suit, but the network paid decades of legal expenses to defend its position. The network finally settled another lawsuit for $85,000 in connection with the show's depiction of Robert Blakemore, then chairman of the Summit County Democratic Party. It was the first settlement in the history of the show.

David Lieberth, now Akron's deputy mayor for administration, worked on Barbuto's 1978 campaign and was the attorney who successfully represented Blakemore. He said Barbuto's misdeeds should be seen as a small part of his history. "Rivera was a hypocrite," Lieberth said, his voice rising twenty-one years after the fact. "He was doing the same thing with women behind the bars in Highland Square that Barbuto was accused of doing in his chambers."

Barbuto was a respected and innovative judge, Lieberth said, but was caught in an ethical sea change.

> *At that time, there were lots of things that were done, that if you looked at them by today's ethical standards would horrify younger people. In those days—not so much. There was a kind of nonchalance about enforcement against people in power.*
>
> *I do think this whole episode in Akron's history requires a rear-view mirror to place the time in context. The conduct of Barbuto and other men like him was conduct they had engaged in for years without fear of retribution. Then the ethic changed and they got caught up.*

Back in the community, Barbuto recovered his health and regained at least part of his reputation as the owner of two successful restaurants, Dodie's in Highland Square and Dale's in Cuyahoga Falls. He retired in 1990.

In 1993, Barbuto was back in the news when he tried to volunteer as a counselor for Summit County Victim Services. Skeptics said Barbuto only wanted the volunteer job to pad his postprison resume in a bid for a pardon from Ohio governor Dick Celeste. Public outrage ended both efforts.

In a 1998 interview with *Beacon Journal* reporter Bob Dyer, Barbuto was anxious to prove he had faced his demons. At the same time, he didn't seem ready to admit any wrongdoing. "I think you have to start off with the premise that I didn't do anything," Barbuto said in the profile. "I could get up in the morning and look in the mirror and not be ashamed of myself."

At eighty-nine, James Barbuto lives alone in the Akron area (as of 2010). He has survived throat cancer and bouts with blood clots and has a feeding tube. According to his daughter-in-law, Camille, Barbuto is well enough to play an occasional round of golf and accompany his family to dinners at the local Italian Society. Though he can no longer eat solid food, he is a dedicated fan of cooking shows, she said.

The former judge declined to be interviewed when contacted for this chapter.

FOOTBALL FLIMFLAM

A man who promised to bring professional sports to Akron was instead responsible for one of the city's most infamous con jobs.

Frank Hurn was a flashy, frenetic, fast talker who favored stark white shirts and sharkskin suits. He often looked like he needed a shave and wore his dark hair in a fat pompadour. People said he made his money building skyscrapers in Chicago and could see the potential beneath a piece of land by just looking at the surface. More importantly, Hurn peddled a dream that nearly everyone in town wanted to buy. In 1967, he came to town as the owner of a minor league franchise of the Continental Football League. By fall, Hurn vowed, the Akron Vulcans would be playing at the thirty-one-thousand-seat Rubber Bowl. It was the only promise Hurn made good on to a team and city that yearned to believe.

As far back as 1920, Akron's passion for football was both deep and tumultuous. That year, the Akron Pros won a game the National Football League considers its first championship, but teams in Akron generally have been short-lived. The Pros became the Akron Indians before folding at the end of the 1926 season. Twenty years later, Chicago Bears owner George Halas opened a minor league team called the Akron Bears to take on the big Bears' overflow; that venture ended after only a year. In 1961, Akron got another shot at football with its first version of the

Discounted student tickets to an Akron Vulcans football game. *Akron* Beacon Journal.

Akron Vulcans—named for the process used to cure rubber—but the team collapsed after losing ten games in row.

To add insult to the city's spotty record of success, Akron literally was sandwiched between constant reminders of sports glory: the Cleveland

Browns to the north and the newly opened Pro Football Hall of Fame in Canton to the south. Akronites were eager to reclaim their piece of sports action. They welcomed Hurn with open arms—and most everyone seemed determined not to examine the newcomer's big promises too closely. Even if Hurn had been seen with more skepticism, it's likely no red flags would have turned up in the beginning.

In April 1967, Hurn and a man named Don Ross really did revive the Vulcans football franchise in Akron when they bought a Continental Football League franchise formerly owned by the Brooklyn Dodgers. The Continental League had been established two years earlier and had seventeen teams in its Eastern and Western Divisions. The league hired players who were cut from National and American Football League teams in the last days of training camp and ran newspaper ads in team cities for open tryouts. The Continental League served as a minor league for the NFL and AFL through 1969.

Hurn's bravado sounded pretty good to Akron. He gained instant credibility when he announced the Vulcans' staff: former NFL all-pro quarterback Tobin Rote signed on as general manager and Heisman Trophy winner Doak Walker was joining the team as head coach. Each man was to be paid $20,000 a year (most folks made about $8,000 annually in those days). Lou Rymkus, a former Cleveland Brown who coached the Houston Oilers in their first championship in the AFL, would be the Vulcans' line coach.

Where the Vulcans traveled, Hurn said his team would go in style. The *New York Times* reported his purchase of a DC-6B, eighty-passenger aircraft that he intended to use to carry players, coaches and a limited number of VIP fans to road games.

In sports pages across the country, Hurn bragged that he had money to burn—at least a half million—to make the Vulcans a reality. "I am prepared to lose money, or else I wouldn't be here," Hurn told the *Beacon Journal*. "The amount I'm prepared to lose? Just say whatever is necessary. Of course, any idiot realizes that a business can't operate at a loss forever."

Maybe Hurn annoyed the football gods. From the very first Vulcans' game, things started to fall apart. The coach's ransom that Hurn said he was prepared to lose—always rumored to be a stake from the Chicago mob—was money the Illinois wise guys apparently were not ready to part with so willingly.

Akron attorney Bob Meeker was the Vulcans' starting guard and offensive captain. He remembers hearing of strange doings at the team's first exhibition game, his first hint that something might be going awry in the Vulcans' front office. Meeker said:

> *My buddy told me this story right after the game, he swears it's true. We had just finished our first exhibition game at the Rubber Bowl against the defending champs, the Orlando Panthers. We had fourteen thousand people there. My buddy was waiting for me outside the locker room. He sees a big Cadillac with Illinois plates pull up. Two guys get out of the big car and walk into the bowels of the stadium…underneath the Rubber Bowl. When they come out a while later, each guy is carrying a big sack. They disappear.*
>
> *The story always was that the mob came to get their money…and as it turned out, receipts for that game never got to the bank.*

It wasn't the last time the Vulcans would have money troubles. Meeker, who was in his second year of law school, had negotiated the team's second-highest salary for himself at $350 a game. He said he never received a nickel. "Those checks bounced higher than this building. Every time we saw Hurn he had an excuse for why we didn't get paid," Meeker said. "One time the money was put in the wrong bank account. The next week he told us the Toronto team was in financial trouble and every other team in the league had to send money to bail them out."

Rote and Walker left after losing three preseason games. The men said they each lost a $30,000 investment and had not been paid their $20,000 salaries. Hurn told the media that the coaches were fired for poor performance.

Around the same time, Hurn was summoned to New York to answer to league officials. He somehow left that meeting with an agreement from the Continental League leaders to restructure $79,000 in debt—money that Hurn owed before the Vulcans set foot on the field for their first regular season game.

Lou Rymkus took over as coach, and Meeker and the rest of the Vulcans hung on for three more matchups with the Charleston Rockets, the Hartford Charter Oaks and the Norfolk Neptunes. Then the Vulcans' players laid down the law: the team sent word to the league that it would not play that weekend's game with the Wheeling Ironmen without payment.

"So this guy, Saul Jacobs, comes to town from the headquarters in Brooklyn, New York," Meeker recalled. "He says the league will pay us $200 cash per man. That sounded pretty good, so we get on the bus and ride to Wheeling. We get off the bus in Wheeling—no Saul Jacobs."

According to Meeker, the Vulcans spent the night in Wheeling, went to church the next morning and suited up for pregame warm-ups before learning that Jacobs was on the other side of the field with the owners of the Wheeling team.

"So that's it. We go off the field, and we're not coming back, and Lou Rymkus, who is about six feet, five inches, goes across the field looking for Saul Jacobs, who is about five feet, three inches—he's going to square off with the guy," Meeker said with a laugh.

With the prospect of a mangled league executive and full stadium of disappointed home-team fans in their immediate future, owners of the Wheeling Ironmen intervened. Essentially, they passed the hat.

"The Wheeling owners come into our locker room, count out $200 in small bills and hand it to each player," Meeker said. "I saw that money go into jock straps, under shoulder pads and into shoes. There was no way we were dumb enough to leave it in that locker room."

At halftime, Wheeling was ahead 28–0. "We went out, and we were obviously a little distracted," Meeker said, "but the game ended 28–27. That was the last hurrah of the Akron Vulcans."

A few days after the last game a local laundry sealed the team's fate when it refused to return the Vulcans' uniforms until the bill for the entire season was paid.

By then, Hurn was in the wind, as police say. News reports at the time accused him of skipping town with about $100,000 in gate and season ticket receipts. Other jilted creditors included Hurn's hotel, Kent State University, which housed and fed the team during a three-week training camp, and, of course, the Vulcans team members and staff.

Summit County officials seize shoulder pads and other assets of the Akron Vulcans after Frank Hurn is charged with fraud. *Summit County Sheriff's Department.*

Hurn's collateral, the value of a supposed commercial heavy equipment company in Chicago, turned out not to exist—even the mailing address was fake. His personal investment in the team was later estimated at $2,000.

Rymkus went on to minor coaching jobs with several NFL teams and taught history to disadvantaged high school kids. As the story goes, he spent days after Hurn left town working the phones at the team office and was successful in placing many of his players with other minor and major league football teams. Rymkus kept calling until the phone line was disconnected; Hurn never paid the bill. Rymkus was a finalist for the Pro Football Hall of Fame in 1988.

Many of the men who played for the Vulcans stayed in town and became local factory workers, businessmen and, in Meeker's case, a former Ohio assistant attorney general.

Hurn returned to Akron—involuntarily—for his sentencing, almost a year after the Vulcans' last game. He pleaded guilty in Summit County Common Pleas Court to eight counts of defrauding an innkeeper of $1,800, which represented the money owed to hotels that housed Hurn and the Vulcans. Hurn was found in Miami after a national manhunt led by local bondsman Whiskey Dick Percoco and the county sheriff. He was sentenced to three years in the Chillicothe Correctional Institution but was released after ten months. He served five years' probation.

The Vulcans were far from Hurn's last run-in with the law. There were incidents involving bad checks and a hit-skip accident in Florida shortly

Frank Hurn in handcuffs being escorted to his court appearance by a Summit County sheriff's deputy. *Summit County Sheriff's Department.*

after his release from probation. And there were other scams in his future. In 1979, Hurn was convicted of selling a coal mine he didn't own and of stealing 240 tons of coal in West Virginia. Court records indicate that Hurn misappropriated and sold the coal he had been hired to process.

Federal prison records show that Hurn was paroled in 1983 from the now-closed Federal Prison Camp at Elgin Air Force Base—the cushy lockup for which the nickname "Club Fed" was coined. His current whereabouts are unknown.

Except for the game against the Wheeling Ironmen, the Akron Vulcans were never paid.

ABOUT THE AUTHOR

Kymberli Hagelberg is a writer, award-winning journalist and native northeast Ohioan. Her work has appeared in newspapers and magazines, including the *Akron Beacon Journal*, the (Cleveland) *Plain Dealer*, the (Biloxi) *Sun Herald* and *Billboard*, and on National Public Radio.

Hagelberg began her writing career as a music critic and entertainment editor. Most of her reporting has focused on politics, business and crime. She holds a bachelor's degree in communication and creative writing from Hiram College. Hagelberg lives outside Akron, Ohio, with her fiancé, three cats and a dog in a happy house with an untidy garden. *Wicked Akron* is her first book.

Visit us at
www.historypress.net